Tim Cortinovis

The
Single-Handed
Unicorn

How to Solo Build a Billion-Dollar Company

The Single-Handed Unicorn

Copyright © 2025 Tim Cortinovis

ISBN: 9798307651278

Thank you for purchasing "The Single-Handed Unicorn", the first step of your journey.

If you want to go further and get your very own questions answered, get in contact with my AI assistant Rick on WhatsApp or on Messenger.

And I would be more than happy if you leave a review on Amazon. Thank you!

CONTENTS

INTRODUCTION

I n *The Grapes of Wrath*, John Steinbeck paints a poignant scene: weary travelers pause along Route 66, gazing at the California horizon. It's a moment charged with tension—a choice between leaning into uncertainty to build something new or retreating from the enormity of it all.

As you pick up this book, I imagine you standing at your own version of that horizon. But your journey isn't westward—it's into the vast possibilities of building a single-handed unicorn enterprise.

I know what you're thinking: *Unicorns? Those billion-dollar enterprises tech giants create with sprawling teams and millions in venture capital?* But what if I told you that, armed with just your laptop, ambition, and the courage to act, you could build something extraordinary—scalable, profitable, and revolutionary—all by yourself? As Anaïs Nin said, "Life shrinks or expands according to one's courage."

You might be skeptical. Maybe you don't have technical expertise or venture funding. Maybe you feel dwarfed by established competitors. But here's the difference: Steinbeck's weary travelers didn't have artificial intelligence.

AI has revolutionized what's possible for solo entrepreneurs. Tools that once required massive teams and budgets are now accessible at little to no cost. Imagine having AI agents that write your marketing campaigns, automate customer service, or even design your products—all at the click of a button. Tools like AdCreative.ai, Bubble, and GPT-based platforms allow you to achieve what once took entire departments.

This is the new horizon: a world where ambition and audacity, not resources, create unicorns.

Efficiency No Longer Wins—Leverage Does

AI isn't just about efficiency—it's about leverage. For the first time in history, one person can harness the power of an entire company. Think of Pieter Levels, creator of Nomad List. With no employees, he used automation and machine learning to build a $400,000-a-year business. He didn't work harder—he worked smarter, using tools that multiplied his impact.

Now ask yourself: how much of your time is spent on manual, mundane tasks? How much more could you achieve with a virtual team of ultra-competent machines at your side? AI doesn't care about your background, location, or resources. It cares only about your ambition and willingness to act.

Your Challenge

This book isn't about dreaming—it's about doing. It's a blueprint for identifying opportunities, automating processes, and building a business that scales beyond what you thought possible. Together, we'll explore:

1. **Identifying problems AI can solve in crowded markets**—because the right battlefield matters.

2. **Automating 80% of operations**—so you can focus on strategy, not busywork.

3. **Launching an MVP in 30 days with no-code tools**—because hesitation kills ideas.

4. **Building passive income streams**—from AI-powered e-commerce to scalable content platforms.

5. **Resilience for setbacks**—because success isn't a straight line.

And along the way, you'll hear real-world stories of people like you—solo entrepreneurs who used these tools to create extraordinary businesses.

Are You Ready?

The tools are here. The opportunities are endless. But the only way to build your unicorn is to start. This book will show you how. The question is: *Will you take the first step?*

CHAPTER 1

THE RISE OF THE
AI-POWERED SOLO ENTREPRENEUR

I n the opening scene of John Steinbeck's **The Grapes of Wrath**, a
dust storm swirls across the American Midwest, symbolizing
both destruction and the single-minded ambition of human
resilience. It is a visceral image of humankind confronting
overwhelming, uncontrollable forces—and yet, finding ways to
adapt, to endure, to thrive. Today, we stand in the middle of a
different kind of storm: a technological revolution swirling with as
much ferocity as Steinbeck's tempest, but this time, it's not
scouring dust; it's code, algorithms, and data. And for the first time
in the history of business, that storm isn't just something we
weather—it's a gale we can harness.

Welcome to the era of the AI-powered solo entrepreneur.

For centuries, innovation has been the dominion of tribes, of
hierarchies, and of armies of people working in concert to produce
economies of scale. Building a company that could change the
world meant access to enormous resources: capital to lease
factories, employees to staff departments, or distribution
networks to ferry ideas and goods into the marketplace. Visionaries
like Henry Ford didn't make industrial history alone; they were
backed by ever-growing hierarchies. Even modern
transformational figures like Jeff Bezos and Steve Jobs scaled their
visions with the help of armies of engineers, designers, and
marketers.

But something extraordinary is happening today. The tools to
achieve similar scale—tools once locked behind corporate walls or
requiring immense capital—are now available to the individual.

They are cheap, or in some cases entirely free. They require less training than ever to wield. And perhaps most astonishingly, they're infused with intelligence—an intelligence so powerful, it often feels like hiring an invisible team that never sleeps, never distracts itself, and never second-guesses your goals.

This chapter will guide you through the tectonic shift that makes this moment possible. We'll dive into why, thanks to artificial intelligence, one person has unprecedented leverage to disrupt industries, create innovation, and build world-changing companies. It's a seismic shift—but whether you thrive in this new world will depend entirely on how you choose to see it.

A Brief Evolution of the Tools of Entrepreneurship

History has a way of sneaking up on us, doesn't it? E-mail killed snail mail long before most people realized how transformative it would be. The gig economy reshaped labor markets before we even found the words to describe it. And it's tempting, here and now, to think of AI tools as little more than a continuation of this trend—a nice upgrade, another step forward.

But this misses the point. AI isn't a step; it's a leap. And to truly understand how massive that leap is, we need to take a look back.

Let's start with the industrial revolution. For the first time, innovation wasn't limited by human muscle—or even human skill. Mechanization turned bottlenecks into breakthroughs, and entire economies were reshaped as industries scaled faster than ever before. But during this era, the vital tool for building the future was physical infrastructure—an asset few individuals had the resources to access.

Fast forward to the personal computing revolution in the 1980s. Suddenly, the tools for creation were...different. A lone programmer with a Commodore 64 could write software that scaled not through factories but through disks or—later—downloads. Bill Gates infamously said his goal was "a computer on every desk and in every home." For the first time, technology was democratizing entrepreneurship—but users still needed technical expertise, and scale still required capital, marketing, and teams.

Then came the internet. Cloud computing. Smartphone apps. Each wave lowered the bar further. You didn't need a factory, but you still needed a co-founder, a couple of developers, a customer support rep, and a web designer.

And now? Now we're standing at the precipice of a world where one person with zero employees can create, operate, and scale—in months what would have once taken teams years to achieve. AI isn't just democratizing entrepreneurship further; it's flipping the power dynamics on their head.

For the first time in history, one person—backed by the right AI systems—has the same leverage as an entire small business.

The Scale of One

Let me introduce you to Laura. Laura is not a mythical figure. She's not one of those cherry-picked outliers we hear too much about in Silicon Valley lore. Laura is an actual solo entrepreneur—a graphic designer from Denver, Colorado—who was laid off from her agency job three years ago. When the pandemic hit, she decided to start her own business, designing packaging mockups for small indie food brands. Before AI tools entered her life, here's what her workflow looked like:

- Sourcing and purchasing stock assets from image marketplaces.
- Hours spent on Photoshop or Illustrator, tweaking packaging mockups.
- A constant battle to juggle client outreach, invoicing, marketing, and design.

It worked, but it was exhausting. She was trapped in a classic trap shared by most small business owners: If she worked tirelessly, she'd eventually reach her ceiling of time as her scarcest resource. When she hit her threshold, she'd hit her revenue cap.

But last year, Laura leaned fully into AI. With tools like MidJourney, DALL-E, and Adobe's Sensei-equipped suite, she automated the creative heavy-lifting. Instead of designing packaging systems from scratch, she used AI to generate tens of concepts instantly—

testing variations and drafts in minutes instead of hours. ChatGPT, layered with custom scripts and prompts tailored for business writing, became her on-demand assistant for handling client emails and generating marketing copy. Another AI tool scrapes market data to tell her which visual trends resonate with audiences **today**, not six months ago.

What happened? Laura's business tripled. Not over years—over months. And it didn't require a team of consultants or extra overhead. It required a mindset shift: the willingness to trust AI-powered tools to behave not just as assistants, but as deeply integrated partners. Laura isn't your stereotypical coder or Silicon Valley insider. She's a one-woman show, using off-the-shelf solutions to beat larger competitors who are still throwing human labor at challenges that no longer require it.

Here's the kicker: Laura hasn't hit a ceiling yet. By automating repetitive and time-intensive parts of her work, she continues to add new projects at a scale impossible to imagine just a few years ago.

Leverage is the New Skillset

Laura is a success story, but she isn't an anomaly. Stories like hers are unfolding every day: podcasters who use AI to automatically summarize hours of audio into shareable clips. Writers who churn out books in weeks instead of years. App developers who prototype, design, and launch tools without writing a single line of code themselves.

This is the moment we're entering: a world where **leverage** is the most vital entrepreneurial skill.

Here's an exercise: If you had an entire team of 100 loyal, highly skilled employees today, what would you do with them? Write down five things that come to mind. Be ambitious. Then ask yourself: What would it cost to build that team? What years of experience would you need? And how impossible would that dream feel?

Now imagine instead those 100 employees are virtual. They don't cost a salary because they're AI-powered. They don't rest, complain, or quit. They do in seconds what would take a human weeks—but they require you to re-think how you own and delegate work.

This is your call to action: How will you think and act if scale is no longer the bottleneck? Will you keep doing what you've always done, squeezing a little more productivity out of the same outdated workflows? Or will you completely reinvent how you approach work—and in doing so, how you approach scaling your ambitions?

Democratizing Ambition Through AI

Imagine, for a moment, you're standing on a leveled playing field—not figuratively, but literally. For centuries, much of entrepreneurship has taken place on a slanted landscape. Capital, knowledge, technology—these resources have historically favored the few, while many others scrambled uphill, pushing great ideas against massive systemic forces. But AI, which levels that terrain, represents the **once-in-a-civilization-level equalizer**.

Consider this: not long ago, if you wanted to create the next billion-dollar startup, you needed significant upfront capital. You had to hire teams of developers to code a functioning product, acquire customers through costly ad campaigns, interpret data via advanced analytics platforms, and manually manage all the day-to-day operations of scaling a company. Think of figures like Steve Jobs, Bill Gates, or Larry Page—they catalyzed revolutionary companies, no doubt, but all within resource-intensive ecosystems.

Now, imagine entrepreneur Janet Smith from Tulsa, Oklahoma—a graphic designer by trade, with a dream of creating an e-commerce platform for custom-made eco-friendly kitchenware. A decade ago, Janet's vision might have required funding rounds or massive loans to hire developers, marketers, and customer service agents. But today? Janet discovers GPT-based tools like ChatGPT for her copywriting—scripting persuasive product descriptions in seconds. She uses platforms like Canva, powered by AI, to design all her branding. Her e-commerce website comes alive, built entirely on a no-code platform such as Shopify or Webflow—so simple that what would have taken a team of coders months now takes her only an afternoon. To market her site, she feeds her target customer criteria into AI-driven ad generators through Meta or Google. And customer service? Janet has AI chatbots handling 80% of the queries.

Janet has no technical co-founder. No team of venture capitalists behind her. No multi-floor headquarters.

And yet, through sheer determination and the accessibility of AI, she creates an online business that nets $2 million in yearly revenue—and all while balancing her life as a single mom.

Does Janet's story seem like fiction? It's not. Stories like Janet's are unfolding everywhere. This is the power of democratized AI. You no longer need to play by the old rules that dictated success required teams, departments, and investors. What matters now isn't the size of your operation but the clarity of your vision and your ability to embrace **intelligent amplifiers**.

This shift is as monumental as the invention of the printing press, which granted humanity the ability to scale knowledge cheaply. Just as the printing press democratized wisdom, AI is democratizing **ability**.

So the question is: Are you willing to step onto this leveled playing field and stake your claim?

From Spark to Scale: Why One Can Do What Once Took Many

In business, there is a long-held belief in the power of scale—that success requires an exponential increase in manpower and resources. But what happens when technology does the scaling for you?

Take, for example, a classic cornerstone of entrepreneurial success: the ability to identify customer pain points and design solutions that directly address them. Traditionally, a company would hire market research teams, product developers, and focus groups to accomplish this. Today, a single individual can achieve the same insights with ease using AI tools like OpenAI, Bard, or Jasper. By inputting relevant prompts, tools like ChatGPT can tell you which products resonate with your core audience, what marketing language will convert, and even how to fine-tune your pricing models for profitability.

Look at the case of Alex, a writer from Portland, who turned his love for fitness into an online empire selling personalized workout programs. At the start, Alex relied on his own expertise to create plans manually, often spending days customizing fitness regimens for clients. This led Alex—burnt out and overwhelmed—to pour his savings into technological solutions. He partnered with developers to build semi-automated customization tools, but it was an expensive "trial-and-error" phase.

Fast forward to the AI-enabled reality we live in today. Alex leveraged AI to automate his business **entirely**. He now uses publicly available AI tools like ChatGPT to generate bespoke workout routines and diet plans in seconds, based on client profiles. He integrates a recommendation engine powered by another suite of AI: it suggests strength training for a recovering athlete or meal prep ideas for a vegan customer. Alex operates with no staff and has grown what used to be 20 clients/month into over 2,000.

Where companies once required human ingenuity applied to every task, now a single mind equipped with AI can architect hyper-efficient workflows capable of scaling **without friction**—it's what I call the compounding of "effective minutes."

So I challenge you to reflect: If you had not ten employees but ten thousand effective minutes of problem-solving in your day—what systems or businesses would you reimagine?

Trailblazers of the AI Age: Breaking the Illusion of Complexity

One of the greatest barriers preventing people from embracing AI is fear—not dramatic fear, like killer robots, but fear of the unknown complexity. Much like someone who's never ridden a bike assumes pedaling and balancing at the same time is a Herculean task, many people see AI as impossibly abstract. They assume they need to learn Python programming or master machine-learning algorithms, and so they hesitate.

But complexity is the great illusion of our time. AI, paradoxically, is making the world simpler.

Take Nathan Barry, creator of ConvertKit. What began as a small side hustle offering email-marketing services turned into a highly successful SaaS company because Nathan saw potential in combining basic automation with great customer relationships. Now imagine a newer generation entrepreneur starting a business like ConvertKit today. Instead of writing code for automation, she could use tools like Zapier powered by GPT to execute workflows with no technical intervention. Instead of launching manually written email campaigns, she could train AI to produce highly personalized sequences tailored to each user's specific behavior.

Or consider Lillian Chen, who entered the healthcare space via a telemedicine startup. In less than one year, Chen leveraged AI to scale a process where incoming clients' symptoms were triaged by an AI-based health assistant—reducing wait times and making medical professionals exponentially more efficient.

Trailblazers like Nathan and Lillian aren't succeeding because they possess secret coding knowledge. They succeed because they recognize AI for what it is—a toolset to amplify their ideas. Their genius is not their proximity to technical expertise but their proximity to courage: the courage to use tools that are available to each and every one of us, even when they're entirely unfamiliar.

So let me ask: Are you making decisions based on what you **think** about AI or based on what you've actually explored?

Turning Fear Into Focus

Many people hear about AI and think, "Won't this automate me out of existence?" It's a reasonable question, but it's the wrong one.

The better question is: "What will I become now that I have freedom—freedom from repetitive tasks, freedom from old constraints?"

In **Fahrenheit 451**, Ray Bradbury wrote that "We need not to be let alone. We need to be really bothered once in a while." Perhaps AI is the thing that's bothering us—and it should! When the ground shifts beneath your feet, it's unsettling. But in the most profound upheavals of history, it's not the people clinging to old rules who succeed. It's the ones asking better questions.

Which industries feel ripe for this kind of reinvention? Which parts of your day feel repetitive, like wasting your intelligence on chores a machine could automate? What dreams feel bigger than you—until you factor in unlimited, scalable assistance?

Those aren't just idle questions. Those are the blueprint for your next chapter.

The Time Is Now

The AI revolution isn't for "the future." It's not even for tomorrow's entrepreneurs. It's for today's. The tools are here. The systems are ready. The only remaining barrier is you—your willingness to see the storm swirling around you not as a threat, but as a force to propel you forward.

It's easy to believe, in today's startup-obsessed culture, that success follows a familiar formula. First, you assemble a team of co-founders—the visionary, the technical genius, the marketing guru. Then, you raise millions of dollars, hire aggressively, and burn cash in a race to "scale." But increasingly, entrepreneurs are rewriting that script. They're proving that it is possible to build billion-dollar ideas alone. No co-founder. No office. No politics. Just a single, motivated individual leveraging technology, obsessing over execution, and scaling sustainably.

So let me leave this first chapter with a question:

If AI can make your dreams 10x more possible, will your dreams be bold enough to match it? Because tomorrow, the solo entrepreneur won't just be capable of scaling revenue or processes. They'll be capable of reshaping entire industries—all on their own.

The groundwork is set. The tools are here. The solo entrepreneur has already risen.

The only question is: Will you rise with them?

CHAPTER 2

REWRITING THE RULES OF SCALE: AI AS YOUR TEAM

Scaling a business has always carried a kind of mythic allure, an entrepreneurial Everest to conquer. The traditional narrative—taught in business schools, portrayed in movies, and upheld by countless "experts"—teaches that scaling requires more: more employees, more infrastructure, more complexity. We've bought into this notion for decades, convinced that progress is a function of how many boots you put on the ground. But what if this thinking is fundamentally outdated? What if scaling no longer means hiring hundreds, building warehouses, or renting floors of office space? What if scaling was no longer about growing **bigger**, but instead growing **smarter**?

The truth is, we're living in a business environment that's undergoing seismic, technological shifts. Artificial Intelligence, once the stuff of science fiction, is now enabling individuals and small teams to accomplish what once required sprawling, global organizations. And in this chapter, we're flipping the script on scale. We'll explore how AI can do more than assist with mundane tasks—it can become your team, your infrastructure, and your superpower, allowing you to build monumental businesses without monumental overhead.

The Fallacy of the Traditional Scale

Think back to Steinbeck's **Of Mice and Men**, where Lennie— enormous and physically capable—endlessly wrestles with his own strength and misunderstood intentions. Traditional scaling, in many ways, mirrors Lennie. Larger teams, expensive infrastructure, and complicated logistics carry immense power but can become unwieldy, inefficient, and expensive without careful management.

Consider this: in 1990, if you wanted to launch a nationwide retail business, you needed physical storefronts in all major cities, warehouse facilities, an army of employees, and a logistical maze of distribution networks. Today? You could build the same reach and revenue potential as a single individual with a Shopify store, AI-driven marketing platforms, and a drop-shipping partner.

Yet, we still hold onto the belief that "bigger is better" when scaling. The cost of this belief is not just financial; it's mental and emotional. Managing a large workforce and complex operations is not only expensive—it also dilutes focus. What's the cost of splitting your attention across salary negotiations, infrastructure expansion, and managing interpersonal conflicts? Is it worth it when there's an alternative?

AI doesn't just reduce costs; it rewires the very definition of scaling. It allows you to scale without **growing**. The question is: Are you ready to let go of the old model and embrace a new way of thinking?

AI as Your Virtual Team: The Core Idea

Now, imagine this: You walk into your office (or open your laptop on your couch), and instead of rows of desks filled with employees, you're greeted by your AI team—each agent hyper-specialized, tirelessly working 24/7, and costing a fraction of what a traditional hire would. Your marketing associate is an AI model designed to target precise microdemographics. Your content creator crafts compelling blog posts, captions, or even video scripts faster than any human could brainstorm. Your customer service representative doesn't blink during rush-hour inquiries at 3 a.m. Because, after all, it's never 3 a.m. to an AI.

This isn't tomorrow's possibility; it's today's reality. Take, for example, copywriting. Historically, businesses have hired experienced copywriters to write product descriptions, email newsletters, or ad scripts. Now, tools like ChatGPT by OpenAI are being used to churn out high-quality, tailored marketing content in minutes. Writers and marketing agencies that once required a team of five or ten employees can now do the same work alone, acting as orchestrators of intelligent machines.

The same goes for customer service. Consider AirAsia, a company that recognized the cost and inefficiency of a sprawling human-staffed call center. They introduced an AI chatbot named AVA that responds to customer queries with astonishing accuracy, handling millions of interactions annually while significantly reducing costs. Would you rather build a customer service empire with thousands of employees sprawled across the globe—or train an AI agent with the ability to serve customers instantly, in multiple languages, and at scale?

It's time to think of AI not just as a tool, but as your team—a collective of tireless, multi-tasking specialists whose skills and reliability exceed human limits in specific domains. So, how can you construct your virtual team, and what tasks can AI take over immediately?

Task 1: Marketing at Scale

Let's start with one of the lifeblood functions of any business: marketing. Marketing is, by its very nature, scalable—each additional email sent, each extra Facebook ad displayed, brings incremental value without the need for proportional infrastructure. But until recently, the **human** elements of marketing, such as audience research, content ideation, and campaign analysis, were time-intensive.

Today, AI tools like Jasper, Writesonic, and Google's Bard can execute these tasks with breathtaking speed. Let's consider an example. Denise, a single mother from Ohio, launched a fitness apparel company with a small budget and big dreams. Leveraging AI tools, she used ChatGPT to build an extensive email marketing strategy, ran Facebook ad campaigns with AdCreative.ai, and created social media videos on Pictory.AI. Within six months, Denise was generating consistent six-figure revenue—all without hiring a social media intern, a graphic designer, or a marketing analyst.

How much of your current marketing spend is allocated toward creative teams or agencies? Could at least some of those tasks be switched to AI platforms, freeing up resources to invest in growth strategies?

Task 2: Content Creation as a Creative Symphony

We live in the era of content. Whether you're a solopreneur or a Fortune 500 CEO, producing engaging, consistent, and relevant content is non-negotiable. But content creation is arguably one of the most labor-intensive processes—requiring writers, editors, graphic designers, videographers, and more. Or at least, it **used to**.

Here's a true story: John was a one-person operation running a YouTube tech channel. Before embracing AI, his content pipeline was bottlenecked by scriptwriting, video editing, and thumbnail design. Then, he introduced AI tools into his workflow. Using ChatGPT, he could write scripts in half the time. AI-powered video editors like Runway ML automated sections of his post-production work, while Canva's AI-generated design templates saved him hours on creating thumbnails. Within a year, John's channel tripled in subscribers, and his income exploded—all without adding a single employee.

Do you struggle to create enough content to meet demand? Could AI be the solution to multiply your output without burning additional human hours?

Task 3: Data Analysis: The Crystal Ball

Remember the days when businesses hired teams of analysts to wade through mountains of data, searching for insights? AI has completely upended this model. Sophisticated analytics tools can now digest vast datasets, identify trends, and generate actionable insights in hours—sometimes minutes.

Take Netflix, for example. While not a "small business" by any metric, Netflix's use of AI to analyze viewer preferences is a model anyone can replicate on a smaller scale. Using machine learning algorithms, they personalize recommendations for 238 million users. But you don't need to be Netflix to put AI data analysis to work. Tools like Tableau and MonkeyLearn allow small businesses to harness the power of data rapidly—for example, by identifying sales trends, spotting underperforming social media campaigns, or even predicting future customer behavior.

How much time are you currently dedicating to analyzing performance data? What if you had smarter tools that did this for you, ten times faster?

The Cost Equation: Humans vs. AI

Now, let's talk about one of the most pragmatic aspects of all this: money. Hiring humans is expensive. Salaries, benefits, training, office equipment—they all add up. AI, by comparison, is scalable at an entirely different cost structure. While a marketing director may cost your business $100,000 annually, subscription AI tools can replicate much of their function for $500 per month.

Think about your business today: What are the roles or tasks where you're spending the most money? If you replaced—or augmented—just one or two of those with an AI solution, how much money could you reinvest into scaling more sustainably?

Challenging the Reader: Will You Rewrite the Rules?

At this point, you're faced with a critical choice. You can cling to the old model of scale—the comfortable stereotype of hiring big teams and creating sprawling infrastructure—or you can embrace the future and scale smarter, not bigger. There is no right or wrong answer, but there is a question you must answer honestly: What kind of business are you building—a machine burdened by its own weight or a sleek rocket designed for speed?

Remember, rewriting the rules starts with letting go of old beliefs. What rules of scale are you still playing by, and which ones can you leave behind?

Building Your Scalable Unicorn

Here's your blueprint: To scale your single-handed unicorn enterprise, create your virtual AI team. Map out the core functions of your business—marketing, content, customer interactions, analytics—and identify the roles where AI can become your ally. Start small. Experiment. Build a workflow where machines handle the repetitive while you focus on creative and strategic growth.

In Steinbeck's world, Lennie never learned to control his strength. But in yours, you have the tools to harness immense power without losing finesse. So, as you plot your path forward, remember that scale isn't about size; it's about capacity. And with AI as your team, your capacity is infinite.

Scalability? It's no longer a question of how big you can grow. It's how intelligently you can deploy the resources at your disposal. Welcome to the new rules of scale.

CHAPTER 3

FROM SOLO
FOUNDER TO SOLO UNICORN

I n the bustling marketplace of ideas, where businesses form, fall, rise, and evolve, the concept of a **solo unicorn**—a billion-dollar business built and operated by a single founder—feels almost mythical. Like chasing Jay Gatsby's green light at the end of the dock, the odds appear stacked against the lone crusader. Conventional wisdom tells us that it takes a village, or at least an army, to build something of enormous scale. But there are those rare exceptions, those solitary visionaries who defy odds, rally technology and strategy to their cause, and turn their dream into a market-disrupting behemoth.

This chapter is about dissecting the anatomy of that rare species of entrepreneur—what I call the **solo unicorn builder**. It's about the discipline, the mindset, the decisions, and, above all, the internal fortitude it takes to transcend the limitations of being just one person and achieve what others can scarcely imagine. If you're reading this chapter, it's not because you're curious—it's because some restless part of you believes you might just be capable of this extraordinary feat too.

So, let's dig in. What makes a one-person idea transform into a billion-dollar entity?

I. The Myth of the Lone Ranger: Is It Even Possible?

In American storytelling tradition, we've always revered the Lone Ranger archetype—the hero who rides toward the horizon, handling every obstacle alone. But in business, this "hero-alone" approach is often discounted. You'll hear critics say: **No one builds**

something big without a team. A fair point... but then there are exceptions.

Take **Sara Blakely**, founder of Spanx. When Blakely started the company in the late 1990s, she was famously a "one-woman operation." She had no formal business experience, no team of advisors, no investors—just $5,000 from her savings, hustle, and raw belief. From cold-calling manufacturers to personally delivering prototypes to Nordstrom buyers, she did it all. Today, Spanx is a billion-dollar brand, and Sara is one of the youngest self-made female billionaires in history.

Or consider **Patreon**, founded by Jack Conte. While the platform eventually scaled into a sizable organization, its earliest success came from Jack himself building a solution to a very personal problem: how creators could monetize their work sustainably. He didn't have a tech team at the time. He didn't have venture capital or a board of directors. All he had was a deep understanding of a pain point and the willingness to create something valuable from scratch. The unconventional solo launchpad of Patreon is a testament to what happens when clarity of vision is combined with relentless execution.

And then there's **Tobias Lütke**, who single-handedly started the code for Shopify. While Shopify eventually grew into a massive undertaking staffed by thousands, its foundation—a platform for small businesses to build online stores—was an intensely personal effort in the beginning. Lütke worked tirelessly alone to create a minimal viable product (MVP) that would later empower countless entrepreneurs.

What these stories reveal is simple: Success favors the solo founder who is obsessively committed to their core idea. Yes, there may come a time to hire employees, bring on advisors, or secure funding, but the gestation period of a billion-dollar business often happens in solitude.

Now ask yourself:

- **Are you willing to endure the sacrifices of building alone?**

- Do you have clarity about what makes your idea worth scaling?

II. The Solo Unicorn Mindset: Discipline Over Everything

If you peel back the curtain on any unicorn founder's life, you won't find "luck" or "genius" alone. What you'll find is an unrelenting devotion to daily discipline. In fact, the ability to **act like a sophisticated team of one** could make or break a solo founder's success.

1. Ruthless Prioritization

When you're one person building for scale, every ounce of energy matters. You simply cannot afford to let distractions seep into your day. Imagine you're a surgeon; every move matters because lives depend on it. Now transpose that same gravitas into entrepreneurship.

Case Study: Nick Swinmurn, Zappos

Nick Swinmurn started Zappos, now a billion-dollar online shoe retailer, with a one-man experiment. He didn't overcomplicate the process or try to build infrastructure to rival Nike. Instead, he simplified ruthlessly: He snapped photos of shoes at local stores, posted them online, and fulfilled orders by buying shoes locally and shipping them himself. That singular focus—validate the demand—allowed him to concentrate his energy where it made the most impact.

Ask yourself: **If I could only invest effort into three tasks this week, which ones would move the needle the most?**

2. The Trial-and-Error Mentality

Unicorn builders don't sit on business plans for years, polishing every detail until they're "perfect." Instead, they ship, test, iterate, and adapt. Every setback is merely a recalibration.

Case Study: Melanie Perkins, Canva

Melanie Perkins started Canva as a solo founder who wanted to democratize graphic design. Her first product wasn't anything near unicorn material—it was a simple, clunky tool targeted at high school students. But she kept refining the process based on user feedback. Canva eventually exploded into a billion-dollar corporation with a one-woman mission front and center.

Key takeaway: Getting it wrong is how you figure out how to get it right. Would you rather fail fast or wonder forever?

3. Building Systems, Not Dependence

A pivotal difference between a solo hustler and a solo unicorn builder is their approach to systems. You can't do **everything** on your own—but what you can control are the repeatable processes that free up your time and energy.

Automation tools, no-code platforms, and outsourcing small tasks allow you to scale yourself. Think of your systems as the "teammates" you create before you hire people. Tools like Zapier and Airtable, or virtual assistants, become extensions of you.

Ask yourself: **What tasks can I automate or delegate to stay focused on my creative genius?**

III. Vision: Why It's More Important Than Capital

Let's sidestep one major barrier to the solo-founder journey: Many believe that without millions in venture capital, they can't possibly hope to achieve unicorn-level success. That belief is simply not true.

Vision, not capital, is the currency of a solo effort. If your solution is deeply meaningful to your target audience, they'll evangelize it—and growth will follow.

Case Study: Julian Shapiro, Demand Curve

Julian built Demand Curve, a marketing company, as a highly profitable, scalable solo enterprise before ever considering expansion. His secret? Obsessing over niche audiences. Instead of creating a generalist agency, he built a blueprint for growth that startups desperately needed. Word-of-mouth marketing fueled his expansion more than any advertising dollar.

Case Study: Joe Gebbia and Airbnb

No Airbnb hasn't always been a billion-dollar idea. But initially? Joe Gebbia, one of the early co-founders, single-handed it all -->

Questions Immediately plugged Doub is the rightframework KEY many sprinkles

CHAPTER 4

THE AI TOOLKIT: BUILDING YOUR ARSENAL

The great American author F. Scott Fitzgerald once wrote that "genius is the ability to put into effect what is in your mind." In many ways, the genius of today's entrepreneur lies not just in their ideas but in their ability to transform those ideas into execution with the right tools. In the roaring digital '20s, we're living through a revolution powered by artificial intelligence—a wave of innovation so profound it's reshaping industries daily. But the entrepreneur who stands out is not necessarily the one who understands every nuance of machine learning or neural networks; it's the one who knows which tools to wield, and when. The tools you choose aren't just instruments—they're extensions of your strategy, energy, and imagination. This chapter is your blueprint to build a world-class AI arsenal.

The Tools that Change the Game

Imagine you're Jay Gatsby from **The Great Gatsby**, standing on the lawn of your mansion, gazing across the bay at the glowing green light—your single, audacious dream. AI tools serve as the bridge to reach those dreams. Whether you're dreaming of building an online empire, creating art at scale, automating your operations, or launching the next billion-dollar business, technology gives you the levers to pull.

But knowing where to start can feel overwhelming. With hundreds, if not thousands, of AI-powered tools emerging, how can you decide what to choose? It's tempting to want to explore them all, like a child in a toy store. Yet success comes not from the breadth of your toolkit but the precision with which you use it.

So, let's start with a question: **What kind of entrepreneur are you?**

Are you the visionary artist with a knack for storytelling? Or are you the analytical organizer, driven by process and systems? Perhaps you're a blend of the two. Your unique style of entrepreneurship will shape which AI tools you choose. Let's explore a collection of tools—and match their strengths to yours.

1. The Communicator's Ally: ChatGPT

Do you ever wish you had a trusted partner who could brainstorm ideas with you at all hours of the day without judgment? That's exactly what ChatGPT feels like. OpenAI's conversational AI is so much more than a chatbot—it is the Swiss Army knife of creative conversations.

Let's take an example: Olivia, a freelance copywriter turned digital entrepreneur. Olivia used ChatGPT to reshape her workflow. She no longer spends hours staring at a blank page while crafting marketing copy for her clients. Instead, she inputs prompts like: "Write a sales email for a sustainable cosmetics brand targeting eco-conscious millennials." In seconds, out comes a polished draft, ready for refinement.

But Olivia didn't stop at emails. She started using ChatGPT to explore branding concepts, taglines, and even content planning for her new side project—a lifestyle blog. ChatGPT became her brainstorming partner, copy editor, and creative muse.

Critical insight for you, the reader: Are you spending time reinventing the wheel every day? Use tools like ChatGPT not just for answers but for inspiration. Think of it less as a machine and more as an endlessly curious intern, there to make you sharper, faster, and freer to focus on big-picture thinking.

2. Midjourney: The Artist's Workshop

You've heard the saying, "A picture is worth a thousand words." For entrepreneurs, it might be worth a thousand sales. Visuals are the lifeblood of branding, marketing, and product design—and

Midjourney, an AI image-generation platform, makes creating stunning, on-brand visuals as simple as typing out a request.

Consider the story of Nico, a solopreneur launching a fashion e-commerce store. With no background in graphic design, Nico had struggled for months to create engaging Instagram posts or promotional banners. Then, he discovered Midjourney. By simply describing what he wanted—"a surrealist depiction of a jogging scene in an urban forest, inspired by Monet's use of light"—the AI created high-quality images that elevated Nico's entire brand aesthetic.

Perhaps you're not in fashion but building a tech application or running a restaurant. It doesn't matter—visual storytelling transcends industry. Midjourney can help you design app mockups, concept art, or even your product packaging, cutting out the need for expensive photo shoots or design agencies.

Challenge yourself: **When was the last time you evaluated your brand's storytelling?** Could the power of visuals make your story more magnetic, your marketing more memorable?

3. Jasper AI: The Writer's Amplifier

Much like ChatGPT, Jasper AI works as a creative companion for crafting content. But where Jasper excels is in creating highly specific, goal-oriented content—whether it's tailored blog posts, catchy ad copy, or even SEO-packed website content.

Picture this: Tanya is launching a niche subscription box service for plant-based snacks. She knows her audience values authenticity, clarity, and sustainability. She doesn't have a massive marketing team, but she subscribes to Jasper. In one afternoon, she generates product descriptions, a landing page script, and ten weeks of engaging Instagram captions—all written with her brand voice infused throughout. Jasper doesn't just write—it adapts, learns, and improves with Tanya's direction.

For you, the entrepreneur building your unicorn: What tasks are you hoarding out of fear that nobody else can do them as well as you? Could it be the case that the right AI tool could do it 80% as well—and save you 80% more time?

4. Zapier and Make: The Gears of Automation

But what good are beautiful words and visuals without efficiency driving your processes? This is where automation ecosystems like Zapier and Make enter the picture. Think of these tools as the Rube Goldberg machines of your business—except instead of convoluted contraptions, they streamline even the most tedious workflows.

Here's how it played out for David. A solopreneur selling handmade leather goods, David was wasting hours every week manually copying order information from his ecommerce platform into Google Sheets, tracking inventory, sending shipping updates to customers, and maintaining social media promotions.

Once David set up Zapier automations, his processes became hands-free. Orders were automatically logged. A trigger would notify him when it was time to replenish inventory levels. Shipping updates sent themselves. Zapier integrated every corner of his business so he could finally step back and focus on what mattered—creating exceptional products.

Automation isn't about replacing you; it's about empowering you. These tools are like the steady hum of the machinery in Willy Wonka's factory, freeing you to dream up your next masterpiece.

5. Pulling It All Together: Your AI Symphony

As you explore these tools, there's an important truth to remember: **no tool can create magic by itself**. The magic comes from you. It's about how you compose your AI symphony—how you integrate tools into your vision and pair them to complement your strengths. Like jazz improvisation, elegant business design is in the interplay between tools and intent.

Consider building your toolkit as an iterative experiment. Start with these questions:

- Are you generating leverage in your business by automating what weighs down your day-to-day operations?
- Are you using creativity-boosting tools to amplify your brand, tell your story, and reach your audience more deeply?
- Are you consistently revisiting whether the tools you've adopted are accelerating your vision—or acting as costly distractions?

Your toolkit will evolve. Today it might include ChatGPT and Jasper for content generation; tomorrow, you might integrate Midjourney or expand your stack with data analysis platforms like Tableau or BigML. The critical skill is to become an entrepreneur who thrives in symbiosis with technology, staying curious, adaptive, and vigilant.

Final Thought: The Gunslinger and the Arsenal

In Stephen King's **The Dark Tower** series, Roland, the Gunslinger, wields iconic weapons, not because they define him but because he's trained to wield them with skill, intention, and focus. This is the metaphor I leave you with as you assemble your AI toolkit. Your tools do not make you an entrepreneur; rather, you are the one who learns to uniquely wield them, crafting your own path to greatness.

So, here's your challenge: turn to the next page. Begin building. Take the first tool, apply it, and then learn your way into the next. With AI as your ally, your mansion across the bay—the green light that drives you—is closer than you think.

CHAPTER 5

HOW TO IDENTIFY BILLION-DOLLAR PROBLEMS THAT AI CAN SOLVE

We live in the Age of Acceleration, a time when the convergence of technology and creativity is rewriting the equations of human potential faster than ever before. Yet amidst this whirlwind of change, one truth remains constant: at the heart of every transformational business stands a worthy problem. But not just any problem—a billion-dollar problem. These are the towering challenges that demand innovative solutions, the seismic disturbances in the fabric of industries. These are the problems that earn businesses not only wealth but also a legacy.

Yet, many entrepreneurs find themselves standing at the edge of this vast ocean, staring into its depths and wondering, **How do I even know which problems are worth solving?**

The answer lies in a methodology, a way of seeing the world that separates the noise from the signal, the minor inconveniences from urgent societal needs. In this chapter, we unlock a simple but powerful framework called the **3Ps: Pain Points, Priorities, Patterns**. It's a formula for uncovering the billion-dollar problems—those headaches that the almighty engine of artificial intelligence (AI) can address, optimize, or obliterate altogether.

Let's dive in.

The 3Ps Framework: A Compass for AI Entrepreneurs

The 3Ps—Pain Points, Priorities, Patterns—serve as your compass in the maze of modern problems. Each P is a lens, offering a different optical clarity for identifying lucrative opportunities that AI is uniquely positioned to solve.

P1: Pain Points—Where Are the Headaches?

Pain points are where businesses and individuals feel frustration, inefficiency, or outright suffering. These are moments when someone groans and exclaims, **"There has to be a better way!"** They could be as grand as inefficiencies in global logistics or as granular as the irritation of toggling between five different apps to organize a team meeting.

Great businesses, from Airbnb to Robinhood, have solved pain points—offering simple, elegant solutions in their wake. What makes pain points ripe for AI intervention is when the solutions involve massive data streams, complex decision-making, or predictive capabilities.

Case Study: Healthcare's Endless Waitlists

Picture this: Jane, a single parent, wakes up with a nagging, chronic pain. She calls her primary care provider, but the next available appointment isn't for six weeks. Desperate for relief but overwhelmed by the convoluted labyrinth of the healthcare system, Jane skips care altogether. This scenario—the friction between patients and healthcare providers—is a multibillion-dollar pain point.

Now, imagine a world where this process is dramatically simplified by AI. Startups like **Zocdoc** are making headway, connecting patients to available doctors in their area. But the opportunity goes deeper. Using AI to forecast appointment cancellations, optimize physician schedules, or triage patient needs could unclog the bottleneck of care at scale. Companies like **Qventus**, which uses AI to improve hospital operations in real time, are tapping into this space. Still, the question remains: who will tackle the remaining inefficiencies in healthcare resource management? The pain point is pervasive, the potential profits enormous.

AI does something profound in pain point scenarios: it takes something chaotic, overwhelming, or slow—and makes it predictable, fast, and seamless.

Ask Yourself:

- In your industry, where are people throwing up their hands with frustration?
- Which parts of their day feel unnecessarily slow, cognitively overwhelming, or bureaucratic?
- What process, if automated or enhanced with AI, would take someone from stressed to elated?

P2: Priorities—What Cannot Be Ignored?

The second P stands for **priorities**—those problems forced upon us by necessity, urgency, or external pressures. While pain points highlight inconvenience, priorities amplify importance. These are the issues governments, industries, or individuals **cannot afford to ignore**.

Consider how the climate crisis has skyrocketed to the top of global agendas: decarbonizing supply chains, optimizing energy use, and managing renewables. These problems moved from **nice-to-solve** to **solve-or-die**. AI is uniquely suited to address these priority issues because it can make sense of impossibly large datasets and tackle complexities at a scale no human brain can handle.

Case Study: Logistics in the Age of E-commerce

It's no secret that e-commerce—and specifically Amazon—has redefined consumer expectations. Two-day delivery feels late. Next-day shipping has become the new standard. But this unprecedented emphasis on speed creates a priority problem: how can businesses meet exponential demand efficiently while minimizing fuel consumption, optimizing routing, and cutting costs?

This is where companies like **Convoy** step in. Convoy uses AI to disrupt traditional trucking by matching shipments to underutilized freight capacity, reducing empty miles and cutting emissions. Similarly, **Flexport** leverages AI to streamline global shipping logistics. The driving urgency here is unmistakable— logistics isn't "nice to improve." It's essential.

And yet, new opportunities abound. Urban last-mile delivery (think delivery drones or sidewalk robots), cold-chain logistics for temperature-sensitive goods (vaccines, for example), and real-time inventory management are areas still brimming with billion-dollar problems. AI, with its ability to forecast future demand, streamline supply chains, and optimize movement, can revolutionize these areas.

Ask Yourself:

- What major challenges are companies, industries, or governments unable to ignore right now?
- Which seemingly impossible goals depend on solving these challenges?
- What piece of this broader puzzle could you own with AI?

P3: Patterns—What Loops Keep Repeating?

Our final P, **patterns**, focuses on those recurring problems that persist across industries, regions, or demographics. Patterns represent systemic inefficiencies or universal pain points—issues AI can tackle at scale.

Think about fraud detection. The actual fraud methods differ greatly between, say, financial payments and health insurance, but the underlying pattern is the same: identifying anomalies in enormous datasets. AI is perfectly suited for such problems because it thrives wherever large datasets must be rapidly understood and acted upon.

Example: Reducing Food Waste

One-third of all food produced globally is wasted. It happens upstream (unsold produce discarded due to forecasting errors) and downstream (restaurants and households tossing out expired food). Look at the pattern: inefficiencies in forecasting demand, tracking inventory, and redistributing unused food are as old as agriculture itself. AI can interrupt this waste cycle.

Startups like **Too Good To Go** help restaurants and grocery stores sell unsold food at steep discounts rather than throwing it away. But imagine a deeper integration where AI predicts demand at micro-levels, ensuring overproduction doesn't happen in the first place. Companies like **Spoiler Alert** are using AI to help manufacturers reduce food overstock. Even smart refrigerators, which track groceries and provide shelf-life warnings, play a role.

The beauty of patterns lies in their universality. They replicate. Solve the problem once, and you can scale your solution thousands—sometimes millions—of times.

Ask Yourself:

- What common inefficiencies have persisted for decades or even centuries?
- Where do problems recur in predictable cycles, creating fertile ground for scalable AI solutions?

The Human Element: A Word of Caution

As you set out to identify billion-dollar problems, here's a critical reminder: AI may be powerful, but it is not magic. Too often, entrepreneurs fall into the trap of chasing shiny, futuristic applications while ignoring the real-world constraints of human behavior and ethics. Just because AI can solve a problem doesn't mean the solution will be adopted—or embraced.

Consider **IBM Watson Health's** struggles to revolutionize cancer care. While AI promised better treatment options, poor data quality and resistance from medical professionals derailed the effort. The lesson? Your AI-based solution is only as good as the data you feed it and the trust you inspire in users.

Identify the Bigger Problem: What is the global pain point that keeps you up at night?

Purpose-driven businesses root themselves in solving problems larger than their immediate markets. Google set out to "organize the world's information" (not just to dominate search engines). Tesla's mission is to "accelerate the world's transition to sustainable energy," not just to sell electric cars.

Ask yourself: What deeper pain point am I addressing with AI that touches millions—if not billions—of lives? What societal or environmental challenge can your technology help alleviate?

3. Dream of the Ripple Effect: What lasting change do you want to create?

Finally, think bigger than the boundaries of your company. Purpose isn't transactional; it transforms ecosystems. Consider how you want your business to impact not only customers, but also industries, communities, and generations.

Here's a real-world example: OpenAI was founded not with the overtly commercial goal of creating a profitable product, but with the purpose of ensuring that AI benefits all of humanity. Every decision—from partnering with academia to safeguarding transparency—aligns with this long-term ripple effect.

A Step-by-Step Exercise to Craft Your Mission

Ready to define your mission? Let's turn your "why" into a guiding star with this exercise. Grab a piece of paper (or, yes, you can use your favorite app, so long as it's not a distraction).

Step 1: Write Your Manifesto

Take 10 uninterrupted minutes to jot down what inspires you most about the intersection of AI and humanity. Don't censor yourself—this isn't the time to be realistic or technical. Write the wildest, most audacious things you hope AI could enable in the world. Forget grammar or structure. Scribble. Dream.

Step 2: Focus Your Scope

Look at what you've written and circle the one line—just one—that feels most urgent. Ask yourself: if you devoted the next ten years to this goal, would you feel fulfilled?

Step 3: Write Your Purpose Statement

Structured like a sentence, it should look something like this:

"We exist to [solve X problem] by [leveraging Y capability] so that [long-term impact]."

For instance:

- "We exist to simplify access to healthcare by using AI to predict disease outbreaks so that underserved communities receive care before crises emerge."

Alternatively, try what I call the **Legacy Filter Question**: After you're gone, what do you hope people will write about your company? This brings you closer to the definitive "why" your business will be remembered for.

Case Study: The Quiet Disruption of Duolingo

Consider Duolingo, the AI-powered language-learning app. At a glance, it's an education platform that uses gamified content and machine learning to personalize lessons. But Duolingo didn't just start with **how** AI can improve learning. It started with **why**.

Luis von Ahn, the founder, grew up in Guatemala, where access to high-quality education was scarce. His mission was never simply to teach languages, but to democratize education globally, to make it both accessible and delightful for everyone, regardless of background. AI became the means for scaling his ambitious vision, continuously tailoring lessons for users worldwide and breaking down barriers between formal education and self-driven curiosity.

When you use Duolingo, what you're engaging with isn't just AI; you're engaging with von Ahn's **why**.

Your Unicorn Thesis

If you find yourself at the edge of inspiration, staring down billion-dollar problems and wondering, **Can I really tackle this?**, remember this: every unicorn business begins with a leap of courage powered by clarity of focus. By harnessing the 3Ps framework, you can build a roadmap—not just for solving a single problem, but for creating a business that scales with exponential precision.

Here's one final exercise before we close this chapter:

1. Write down three pain points you or those in your industry experience regularly.
2. Identify at least one priority problem for your industry or society as a whole.
3. Spot a recurring pattern—something you've seen across multiple contexts—that AI might solve.

Choose one, dig deeper, and start building. Because at the core of every unicorn enterprise lies a decision: the courage to wager your future on a problem worth solving.

Asking the Hard Questions

Before we conclude this chapter, I challenge you to grapple with these questions:

- What would your enterprise continue to stand for even if AI were no longer relevant tomorrow?
- Who benefits most from what you're creating—and why do they matter to you?
- If your business succeeds wildly, what will the world gain?

The answers may not arrive instantly. But if you sit with these questions long enough, you'll find yourself stepping closer to your green light—a purpose so inspiring, it'll keep your vision steady even as the pace of technological advancement accelerates.

Now, reader, I ask: **Which billion-dollar headache will you solve?**

CHAPTER 6

DESIGNING YOUR
AI BUSINESS BLUEPRINT

What if I told you that your business is like building the Dewey Decimal System all over again, but instead of organizing books, you're organizing opportunity? Every shelf, every stack in that infinite library must be purposeful, aligned, and designed to solve a specific problem for your patrons. In this chapter, we'll tackle one of the most critical steps in your AI-powered venture: creating a business blueprint. This blueprint is your compass, your map, your GPS — and without it, your solo enterprise can easily veer off course. To paraphrase Mark Twain, "If you don't know where you're going, any AI model will get you there...but it might not be where the customer needs you to be."

Begin with Empathy: What's the Story You're Solving?

Before diving into the "how," let's refocus on the "why." Why does your business exist? Who does it serve? As we explore methods to create your AI business blueprint, I'll ask you to step back and think of your customer not as a data point, but as a character in need of transformation. This means putting every spreadsheet, every algorithm, and yes, even every GPT prompt, on pause for a moment.

Imagine your customer is the protagonist in **The Grapes of Wrath**. They're on a journey. Maybe they're escaping drought (a professional challenge). Maybe they aspire to build a dream (launching an idea, streamlining their production, learning a skill more efficiently). AI is your opportunity to build the roads, the bridges, and the roadside diners they need to traverse the vast deserts of uncertainty.

Let's break this process into actionable steps, and to ground this in the real world, we'll explore examples and metaphors to show you the way.

Step 1: Use the Business Model Canvas to Visualize the Blueprint

The Business Model Canvas may sound abstract, but its beauty is its simplicity. Conceived by Alexander Osterwalder, this one-page visual framework helps you clarify the nine essential building blocks of your venture:

1. **Customer Segments**: Who are you creating value for?
2. **Value Propositions**: What problem are you solving, and how?
3. **Channels**: How can you deliver your product to your audience?
4. **Customer Relationships**: How do you acquire, nurture, and retain customers?
5. **Revenue Streams**: How will you monetize your solution?
6. **Key Resources**: What tools, technologies, or partnerships will power your business?
7. **Key Activities**: What daily actions will deliver your value proposition?
8. **Key Partnerships**: Who can complement your skills or bolster your offering?
9. **Cost Structure**: What will it take to make it all work?

Here's an example:

Sarah, an independent UX consultant in San Diego, used generative AI to create **CopyCraft**, a tool that designs instant wireframe copy for user interfaces. Her Value Proposition was clear: speeding up the copy creation process for designers under tight deadlines. Her Key Resources included her tech stack (GPT-4 API) and an online course she created to teach users how to maximize the tool. But her secret sauce was her focus on Customer Segments. Instead of targeting everyone in the design industry, she narrowed her audience to freelance UX designers and startups; folks who often didn't have dedicated teams for these nitty-gritty tasks but faced immense pressure to scale.

Meanwhile, Sarah planned her Channels with precision. She listed herself on Gumroad, organically expanded on Product Hunt, and hosted free webinars on LinkedIn Live. Sarah's Cost Structure? Sleek and lean. A $12/month GPT-4 API subscription and the hours she spent refining her tutorials.

Her Revenue Stream? Simple. A $39 monthly subscription for premium users on CopyCraft. Sarah wasn't inventing AI. She wasn't creating a unicorn in the garage overnight. But she was solving a hyper-specific problem for a hyper-specific audience — and building her empire block by block.

Now ask yourself:

-   Who is the person most desperate for your AI-powered solution right now?
-   Is your problem clear enough that they'll immediately say, "That's exactly what I've been looking for"?
-   Where can you visually map your idea within each of these nine blocks?

Step 2: Think Lean and Get Out of the Building

The second foundational component of an AI business blueprint comes from Eric Ries' **Lean Startup** methodology. Here's the shorthand: design small, fail fast, and learn even faster.

Jack London wrote in **To Build a Fire** that ignoring the environment is a fatal flaw. The same applies to your business. You may be excited to code, to experiment, and scale your AI tool right from square one — but if you don't step out into the proverbial snow, feeling its weight from a customer's perspective, you're setting yourself up for failure before you've properly begun.

The core idea of Lean Startup is a Minimum Viable Product (MVP): test the smallest, most basic form of your concept as early as possible. In the world of AI businesses, this could mean launching an extremely stripped-down interactive demo. Resist the temptation to automate everything from the very beginning.

Zain, an IT freelancer in New York, wanted to help small businesses with limited budgets replace their time-consuming customer support FAQs with a chatbot. His initial idea was to build a massive, fully customizable chatbot solution that handled not just FAQs, but sales queries, order updates, and refunds. It was, frankly, overwhelming. He quickly realized he was designing Rome before even asking if anyone wanted a forum!

So Zain pivoted. His MVP became a one-page form. Users typed in their top 10 FAQ questions, and Zain manually fed them into ChatGPT to create chatbot scripts. It wasn't scalable. It wasn't perfect. But small shops loved it, because it provided a solution quickly and inexpensively — one that saved them hours of replying to redundant emails every week.

After six months, Zain understood his customers' real problems — or rather, their deeper transformations. It wasn't about solving FAQs; it was about automating workflows so they could spend their afternoons closing sales or planning expansion strategies.

Lean isn't just about iteration. It's about humility. This begs the question:

- Have you built enough of your product to test whether customers even care?
- If you made your solution 90% LESS functional, could you still deliver value?
- Is your product solving what THEY want — or what YOU want them to want?

Step 3: Storyboard the End-to-End Customer Journey

Here's an exercise: Imagine you're reading a Jonathan Franzen novel like **The Corrections**. The tension between characters — a frustrating spouse, a wayward child — feels painfully human. Your customer's experience with your product should feel that **visceral**, that clear. There's an entire human process wrapped around how they first encounter you, how they use your AI solution, and how they feel long after implementing it.

To storyboard this, think like a screenwriter planning a movie about your customer journey.

- **Scene one:** Where do they first discover your tool? Are they frustrated, curious, skeptical?
- **Scene two:** Do they spend a week on your landing page, or does their decision take 15 minutes?
- **Scene three:** What happens the first time they **really** experience the value? Are they amazed, mildly satisfied, or a little confused?
- **Final scene:** After using your solution for three months, are they begging their colleagues to try it too, or is it gathering digital dust?

Let's look at Airbnb for comparison. In its earliest stage, its founders storyboarded every element of their customers' journey: from the photos hosts would upload, to how travelers trusted strangers enough to sleep in their homes, to those inevitable awkward conversations when guests and owners first met in the kitchen. They built the whole story **before** writing a single line of code.

With your AI business, your customer's story might revolve around personalization. For example, if you build an AI-powered video editor for content creators, your storyboard might focus on how stressful it is for a TikToker to edit 30-second clips at lightning speed. If your AI takes that pain away, how will that empowering transformation feel in their journey? Will you save them time, energy, imagination — or something even deeper, like self-confidence?

Step 4: The AI Advantage — Amplify Linked Benefits

Technology is often seen as the engine of innovation, but AI is unique: it amplifies the **emotional** fulfillment customers get from your solution in ways traditional tech does not. Consider these superpowers:

1. **Speed**: AI tools deliver value exponentially faster than humans.

2. **Scale**: One person, like you, can now serve thousands.
3. **Personalization**: The core of AI is its ability to customize at scale.

An exceptional example of these powers in action comes from Chandu, a math tutor in Ohio. Using OpenAI's Codex API, Chandu created an app for parents called **Homework Helper**. Middle school students uploaded their math problems, and the app gave them not just answers but step-by-step **explanations** in Chandu's voice — recording bits of advice he pre-programmed, like "Always check your work first!"

But here's the twist: that wasn't Homework Helper's real value. Chandu also included an AI-powered **parent dashboard**. A weekly digest sent parents insights, not only about their child's performance, but also suggestions on how to encourage struggles as "learning moments." Parents felt included as partners in their children's education, not just passively observing.

The AI amplified not just the efficiency of homework help, but the emotional resonance of family dynamics. If Zain from earlier solved FAQs, Chandu solved **family tension**. That's the next-level promise of AI business design when done right.

Step 5: Pressure-Test the Blueprint

Ask yourself today: If your business failed in the next three months, why would it fail? Would customers say it missed the mark on pricing? Feature overload? Poor onboarding? If you can imagine those critiques clearly, you've already built the first draft of your blueprint. Remove the imagined blockers NOW.

A final exercise for you: Sketch your own business model using the steps in this chapter. Write your customer's story as though writing a novel. Challenge your assumptions like Thoreau criticized society. And most importantly, remember: an AI unicorn isn't about having all the answers. It's about asking the boldest, most human-centric questions.

Keep building.

CHAPTER 7

THE LEAN AI STARTUP: BUILD SMALL, SCALE BIG

Imagine for a moment that you're holding a rough, unpolished stone in your hand. It's not much to look at, maybe even dismissed by others as a mere pebble. Yet, with time, care, and careful chiseling, it transforms into something dazzling—a diamond. In many ways, building a successful AI startup is no different. You start with what seems like the simplest version of an idea—a rudimentary version of the grand vision that keeps you up at night. You deliver it into the market with one overarching goal: to allow your customers to help you refine it into a gem. Welcome to the foundational philosophy of the Lean AI approach: Start small, iterate relentlessly, and scale big.

The Lean AI approach isn't a throwaway buzzword or a corporate catchphrase; it's a battle-tested framework that has birthed billion-dollar unicorns, reshaped industries, and transformed basement startups into household names. In this chapter, we're going to dive deep into the principles and practicalities of this approach. We'll explore how you, as a founder, can apply it to build your own AI-powered enterprise—from a scrappy minimum viable product (MVP) to a scalable, profitable, world-changing business.

But before we leap into action, let's challenge the oft-romanticized notion that you need to have it all figured out—the perfected algorithm, a sprawling dataset, or the ultimate killer app—before stepping into the arena. Spoiler alert: You don't. You just need the pebble and a powerful commitment to chisel away every single day.

The Art of Starting Small: The Role of the MVP

The minimum viable product (MVP) is where it all begins. But let's clarify something right now: AI-powered MVPs aren't your typical tech prototypes. They're not flashy. They're not over-engineered. And they certainly aren't perfect. They are the distilled essence of your dream—just enough functionality to demonstrate value to your target audience while being barebones enough to collect feedback on what matters most.

If the Lean Startup methodology popularized by Eric Ries taught us anything, it's that MVPs are experiments, not monuments. And in the context of AI startups, this principle holds an almost sacred status. Why? Because AI is not deterministic; it's probabilistic. It's messy, iterative, and often unpredictable.

Instead of waiting two years to build the "perfect" recommendation engine or chatbot, your goal is to launch a version that works "just well enough." Start with something people can talk to, interact with, and critique—even if it only solves 10% of their problem. It may feel counterintuitive to release something flawed, but remember, no masterpiece exits its creator's hands intact. Hemingway famously rewrote the final pages of **A Farewell to Arms** thirty-nine times. Your AI product deserves the same patience for reinvention—with one key twist: You're writing it directly with (and for) your audience.

Let me introduce you to Tristan, the founder of a now-booming AI startup that develops AI-driven dietary plans. When he first started out, Tristan didn't have a robust AI model. He didn't even have good datasets or a scalable interface. What he had was a simple Google Form. Customers would input basic information about their dietary preferences and restrictions, and Tristan would manually process the data, simulating what an AI algorithm **might** do in the future. It wasn't glamorous, but it worked. Feedback poured in, patterns emerged, and eventually, he trained a custom AI model based on real-world data that customers had willingly offered to him. Today, his platform seamlessly scales to tens of thousands of users, but the foundation—his MVP—was decidedly scrappy.

What's the take-home message? Your MVP isn't just a product; it's the spark that lights the bonfire, the little snowball rolled at the top of the hill. It's the starting point for a much larger conversation between you and your users—a conversation you **cannot afford to avoid**.

Build, Then Learn—Fast: The Feedback Flywheel

Let's talk about iteration, the lifeblood of the Lean AI process. The moment your MVP hits the market, you need to be able to listen, adapt, and improve—on high-speed repeat. For a moment, consider Harper Lee's **To Kill A Mockingbird**. Lee's fictional characters, particularly Scout Finch, teach us that wisdom is born of observation. Scout learns by attentively watching those around her—absorbing lessons about human nature, morality, and justice. Likewise, your model will learn best by engaging with the real world—specifically, your customers.

The feedback cycle is where great companies distinguish themselves. When OpenAI dropped its GPT-3 powered interface, they didn't claim it was perfect. They leaned into user feedback— learning how individuals used it, abused it, and even coaxed it into producing completely unexpected outputs. By observing, they identified weaknesses and strengths. Over time, iterations made the tool smarter, safer, and more commercially viable. Their willingness to release an imperfect product, listen intently, and improve continually was critical to their success.

Ask yourself: Have you approached your product development with the humility to be wrong? With the discipline to listen? With the flexibility to pivot?

A beautiful example in the AI space is a lesser-known startup that decided to build an AI-driven essay grading system for university professors. Their MVP, initially crude, misjudged nuances like sarcasm or context. But the founders weren't deterred. They sent their MVP out anyway and actively encouraged teachers to highlight where it failed. They didn't just collect feedback; they treated feedback as oxygen.

Over a grueling six months of refining algorithms—not in solitude, but in relentless communication with actual users—the system grew exponentially more accurate. Today, the business is not only profitable but respected as solving a real-world pain point in higher education—a platform that professors genuinely rely on. Their success hinged on their audacity to release, their openness to criticism, and their obsession with bettering their product.

The lesson? Launch your flawed gem. Let the market critique it. Build the feedback flywheel and let customers polish what you initially cobbled together in a makeshift workshop.

Don't Just Solve Problems—Nail One

There's another temptation you must overcome as an AI founder: the urge to overreach. It's easy to get swept away by the promises of AI—a technology that, many will argue, can do almost **anything**. But the danger lies in trying to pursue everything and solving nothing well.

Mark Zuckerberg famously told his team in the early days of Facebook to "figure out one thing you do better than anyone else and work on it relentlessly." This ethos should become your mantra as an AI entrepreneur. Your MVP does not—and cannot— do everything. Your algorithms do not—and cannot—solve every issue. Stay laser-focused on solving **one** pain point for your customers, and do it in such a way that they can't imagine life without your solution.

Take the story of Clara Labs, the AI-powered scheduling assistant. In its earliest iteration, Clara didn't try to build a universal assistant. Instead, it tackled one precise problem: email-based scheduling. By focusing narrowly, the team was able to master natural language processing (NLP) specifically for email exchanges. They trained their AI to pick up nuances in sentence structure, formalities, and even cultural sensitivities in scheduling etiquette. Early adopters became evangelists because Clara didn't just solve "any problem"—it nailed one problem better than anyone else.

So I ask you: What is your "one problem"? What pain point could you solve today that would make customers say, "This changes everything"?

Scaling Big: Weathering the Transition

Once you've delivered value through your MVP and iterated based on feedback, scaling your business becomes the next step in your journey. But make no mistake: Growth is more perilous than most assume. It's not uncommon for startups to collapse under the sheer weight of their ambitions, spending unwisely on cloud-computing costs, hiring prematurely, or overcomplicating their strategies.

One of the greatest challenges for AI startups at scale is managing performance. It's easy to get lulled into security when a model works for 100 users, only to discover that it crashes under the weight of 10,000 simultaneous interactions. Glean lessons from Netflix here. In its early days of streaming, Netflix underwent rigorous load tests for its recommendation algorithms, testing user experience when servers were strained or predictions faltered. This foresight saved them when their subscriber base expanded exponentially.

Your AI model must be scalable by design. Start thinking early about how to structure for success, yet resist over-engineering. Plan for the bonfire, but don't snuff out the ember in your rush to build one.

The Challenge Ahead

As you read this chapter, you may feel both inspired and daunted. Starting small isn't glamorous, and the road from MVP to scalable success is littered with missteps and setbacks. But remember this: The startups that endure—the ones that evolve into single-handed unicorns—aren't the ones that **solve everything** or **build perfectly from day one**. They're the ones that **adapt**, that **listen**, that **commit to the process**.

So let me ask you, entrepreneur: What are you chiseling away at today? What raw, unpolished idea can you set loose into the world, flawed yet capable of remarkable transformation? And when that idea begins to shine, will you have the patience to nurture it, the humility to learn from it, and the courage to scale it?

The Lean AI approach is the sharpest tool in your entrepreneurial toolkit. Use it wisely—not to rush the process, but to refine it one deliberate step at a time. Start small, iterate relentlessly, and, when the time is right, watch it scale big.

Because diamonds, after all, don't start perfect—they start as pebbles. Keep chiseling.

CHAPTER 8

HOW TO AUTOMATE 80% OF YOUR BUSINESS OPERATIONS

Automation is no longer an innovation—it's a necessity. In the modern world of business, time is not just money; it's lifeblood. The enterprises that learn how to automate effectively aren't just cutting costs or streamlining processes—they're building bulletproof systems that free up cognitive and operational bandwidth to focus on creativity, strategy, and growth. This chapter will walk you step-by-step through the practicalities of automating 80% of your business operations.

To start, let's get something very clear: automation doesn't mean relinquishing control. That's one of the biggest myths in entrepreneurship. Automation means you're delegating everything repetitive, predictable, and mundane to machines so you can focus on what truly matters—the human side of your enterprise, the big ideas, the deeply strategic challenges. Picture Gatsby's elaborate, self-sustaining social machine in **The Great Gatsby**. Automation is not unlike the orchestra behind Gatsby's parties. It keeps the champagne flowing so he can focus on the grand performance. Except in this case, the champagne is a near-endless release of mental and physical energy into pursuits that yield exponential value.

The True Value of Automation: Why Entrepreneurs Must Adopt It Now

Think about the last time you managed a task that felt monotonous yet necessary. Maybe it was manually onboarding a new customer, inputting their details into your CRM, sending them a welcome email, and directing them toward the next steps. Maybe it was reconciling last month's accounting or answering yet another frequently asked question in customer emails. It's the entrepreneurial equivalent of mowing your lawn when a professional landscaper is available for $20. Spending your finite time and creative energy on tasks like these is akin to stealing from your future self.

Automation is your personal landscaper—but better. It ensures that repetitive activities happen automatically and at scale, with more accuracy than even your best employee. Cisco conducted a study that showed automation can save businesses up to 20 hours per week for tasks related to data entry, email management, and reporting alone. That's more than two full workdays!

But automation doesn't stop at time-saving. It helps safeguard consistency, a critical but often underappreciated aspect of building trust with customers and employees. McDonald's fries taste the same in New York and Tokyo because their processes are automated to within an inch of perfection. When systems are automated, the margin for error shrinks while the potential for growth balloons. Now, how might you apply this same principle to your business?

Step 1: Identifying the 80% That Can Be Automated

Before we analyze tools or strategies, the first challenge is clarity: what 80% of your business operations are ripe for automation? Harvard Business School professor Clayton Christensen once said, "A good theory doesn't only explain what has happened; it predicts what will happen." The same logic applies to your processes. You need to identify the repeatable, predictable workflows in your business.

Here's a breakdown of areas most businesses can automate:

- **Customer Service**: FAQs, live chat responses, ticketing systems.
- **Marketing**: Social media scheduling, email marketing campaigns, lead nurturing.
- **Sales**: Lead scoring, follow-up sequences, proposals.

- **Operations**: Inventory management, file organization, report generation.
- **HR**: Onboarding, payroll, time tracking.

Take a quiet hour to audit your week. Keep a notebook nearby (or a voice memo app open) and document every task you feel drains time and energy. By the end of the week, you'll have a clear list of tasks waiting to be automated. Ask yourself: "If I were to magically step away for 30 days, which of the processes on this list could a piece of software reasonably manage without me?"

Metaphorically speaking, this is like identifying the weeds in your garden of creativity—removing them gives the flowers (the high-value, strategic work) more sunlight and resources to grow. The seeds of your single-handed unicorn enterprise are planted here.

Step 2: Building Your Automation Stack

Now that you know **what** to automate, the next step is determining **how**. The key is creating an automation stack, a robust set of tools that work together to handle the heavy lifting.

Example 1: Automating Customer Communications

Let's imagine you're running a boutique e-commerce empire selling artisanal leather wallets. Customer inquiries flood your inbox daily. "Do you ship internationally?", "What's your return policy?", "Can I get a custom engraving on my wallet?" You realize 70% of inquiries are repetitive.

Enter **AI-driven chatbots** like Intercom or Drift. These platforms use natural language processing to handle basic customer questions seamlessly. You train them with a robust FAQ database, setting them free to reply instantly to questions. Suddenly, manual replies drop by 80%. For the 20% of inquiries that require the human touch, the bot flags a representative with detailed context, saving time for customers and employees alike.

Now, let's integrate. Pair this chatbot with email automation through platforms like Mailchimp or Klaviyo. Once a customer makes a purchase, they receive a series of pre-built emails—the

"Welcome" email, followed by a "How to Care for Your Wallet" tutorial, and later, a "Thank You/Leave a Review" email. This drip campaign grows your rapport while building brand loyalty—and it's 100% hands-off.

Example 2: Streamlining Employee Onboarding

You hire a new virtual assistant to help with backend operations. Typically, onboarding feels like a slog, rife with repetitive emails, document sharing, and account setup. Here's how to automate the entire process:

1. Use a workflow automation tool like **Zapier** to trigger a welcome email as soon as you sign the contract.
2. Involve **HR tools** like BambooHR or Gusto, which automatically assign the employee onboarding checklist, complete with deadlines and linked learning resources.
3. Pair it with **knowledge management platforms** like Notion or Trainual, so the new hire instantly gains access to SOPs (standard operating procedures) and training materials.
4. Automate system permissions through tools like LastPass or Okta to give the employee credentials without manually managing passwords.

Your new team member logs in on Monday morning with all resources at their fingertips, ready to hit the ground running. Meanwhile, you're sipping coffee, unbothered by the drudgery of micromanagement.

Step 3: Layering AI for Smarter Decision-Making

Automation is good. Intelligent automation is transformative. Modern AI tools don't just expedite tasks; they predict, recommend, and adapt, ultimately behaving like an extension of you.

Case Study: Predicting Sales Trends with AI

Imagine you're running a SaaS platform for fitness coaches. You notice monthly revenue fluctuates, but you're unsure why. Here's where platforms like **HubSpot** and AI-enabled CRMs step in.

First, integrate AI that tracks user interaction on your website. Let's say it predicts that visitors who view your pricing page twice are 3x more likely to convert during promotion seasons. From there, you pair the data with email marketing automation. The system automatically sends promo codes to leads that meet those patterns. Your promotions now behave like laser-guided missiles, surgically precise and powered by intelligence.

Furthermore, AI can analyze past data to forecast subscription churn. Tools like Pendo flag accounts at risk of cancellation and even suggest retention strategies. Automation doesn't just work in the present; it builds you a predictive map for the future.

Step 4: Measuring and Refining Automation ROI

Every powerful system needs a feedback loop. Without measuring a process's efficacy, you risk spending more time fixing a broken automation than the task itself would've required.

Begin with this: define success metrics for each process. Are you automating customer support? Look at response time and resolution time. Automating marketing? Measure email open rates and click-throughs. Tools like Google Analytics, Tableau, or even Slack integrations can passively report ROI to your dashboard.

Go further by bringing humanity back into the equation. Ask employees how automation has impacted their day-to-day work. Are customers finding interactions more seamless? Use surveys and employee feedback to validate the quality as well as the quantity of the outcomes.

Finally, remember automation is a perpetual motion machine—it grows with refinement. Treat every failure or hiccup as a lever to improve processes.

Challenging the Unicorn Within You

When you strip the non-essential tasks from your daily scope, a question emerges: what will you focus on instead? Forget tasks for a moment. What is the deeper purpose of your business? Where will you invest the time you win back?

Automation isn't just operational—it's existential. It forces you, as the entrepreneur, to confront yourself. Will you use this newfound freedom to revolutionize your industry? Will you explore new markets, deepen customer experiences, or rethink the impossible?

Conclusion: The 80% Rule of Automation

Achieving 80% automation doesn't mean you're coasting; it means you've built a self-sustaining engine that paves the road for limitless growth. From customer support bots that never sleep to AI-driven sales strategies that predict tomorrow's trends, every aspect of your business is a candidate for leverage.

But remember, while you're automating the repetitive, hold sacred the 20% that should never be automated: creativity, connection, innovation, vision. These are the domains your unicorn enterprise will thrive on. Let the machines hold the line so you can soar overhead.

CHAPTER 9

MASTERING TIME
MANAGEMENT WITH AI

There's an old adage you've probably heard: "Time is money." But for the solo entrepreneur, time is far more precious than money; time is life itself. Money can be gained and lost, earned and borrowed, but time is a resource with razor-thin margins and no ability to be replenished. It's finite, unforgiving, and yet—for those who master it—unparalleled in its capacity to catapult your business to greatness.

The tech writer Kevin Kelly once said, "You'll be paid in the future based on how well you work with robots." Today, however, it's not just robot arms in warehouses or driverless cars disrupting transportation. The robots helping us today are smarter, more deeply embedded in our lives, and quietly revolutionizing how we manage our most precious resource: time. Artificial intelligence (AI) isn't simply the preserve of billion-dollar tech CEOs. It's democratized and within reach of anyone with an internet connection. For the solo entrepreneur striving to build a one-person unicorn business, AI represents something akin to a cheat code—if you're willing to embrace it.

In this chapter, we will explore how solo entrepreneurs can reclaim hours—literal hours—every single day through AI time management tools. You'll not only learn actionable strategies but be gently challenged to confront your own limiting habits about how you spend your time.

Let's start by rewiring your perspective on time itself.

The Illusion of Time Control (Why We're Our Own Worst Enemies)

Picture a solo entrepreneur—let's call her Elena. She has a talent for graphic design and early on in her freelance career, she gathered enough clients to consider herself successful. But as her business grew, Elena constantly felt like she was losing control of her hours. Every day became a chaotic whirlwind of client calls, proposal writing, project deadlines, and the mundane tasks of invoicing and email replies.

She thought time blockers on her calendar would help. They didn't. She tried multitasking—completing a design mockup mid-conference call or responding to emails while attending webinars. That didn't work either. At the end of every day, she'd collapse into bed feeling exhausted but unproductive, unsure of where all her time had gone.

Elena's predicament isn't unique. If you've ever found yourself cutting into personal time or burning out while trying to keep your business afloat, we need to name the villain in the room: **you don't manage your time as much as you think you do**.

The myth of multitasking has encouraged us to believe we can do everything, all at once, with the same intensity and focus. Neuroscientist Earl Miller from MIT debunked this myth long ago—our brains don't juggle; they switch. Every time you shift from writing an email to scrolling Instagram to tweaking your website, you're burning mental energy on task transitions. The result? Inefficiency, mistakes, and a rapidly depleting tank of cognitive fuel that you really can't afford.

This constant state of reactive busyness isn't just misuse of your time; it's akin to pouring water into a bucket riddled with holes. You'll never fill it.

But here's where AI comes in—your virtual cork for every leak in the bucket.

The AI Saviors for Your Schedule

AI's role in time management is analogous to hiring an all-star personal assistant who doesn't sleep, doesn't need coffee breaks, and never suffers from Monday brain fog. Let me introduce you to a few tools that every solo entrepreneur should consider adopting. We'll focus on three categories: scheduling, task management, and prioritization.

1. AI Scheduling: Automating the Art of the Calendar

Here's a brutal truth: negotiating schedules wastes an obscene amount of time. "Does 3 PM work for you? No? How about Thursday at 10 AM?" Multiply this by five clients and your productivity plummets. AI-powered tools like **Calendly**, **Motion**, and **Google Calendar with AI enhancements** take this burden off your plate.

Let's revisit Elena. She started using Calendly, allowing her clients to book calls during specific windows of her choosing. But she didn't stop there. She added Motion—an AI tool that dynamically reorganizes her workday based on her priorities, email volume, and deadlines. If a client canceled a call, Motion seamlessly reassigned that time to complete the most high-value task on Elena's to-do list. Over a month, she tracked her time and realized she gained an extra **7 hours a week**—the equivalent of almost an entire day—for deep, focused work.

Now, close your eyes for a moment and think about this for your own life. What would you do with seven extra hours a week? Write a pitch for that dream client? Launch the podcast you've been putting off? Or, perhaps, finally take a guilt-free step away from your laptop for some overdue personal time?

2. Task Management: The Power of AI Co-Pilots

Many entrepreneurs fall victim to what I like to call "productivity theater"—spending hours organizing a to-do list but never actually tackling the items on it. Traditional task management tools, like trello boards or sticky notes, operate as static lists. AI, however, brings active intelligence into the equation.

Tools like **Todoist's AI** and **Notion AI** can do more than just list your tasks. They can group them by context, prioritize them by urgency versus importance (think Eisenhower Matrix logic), and even suggest which hours of the day you're statistically more likely to complete them based on your historical work patterns. When every task is in its optimal place, ideas flow effortlessly. By thinking less about chores and more about creative execution, AI liberates you to focus on your unique value proposition.

Use a metaphor from literature to think about this: remember Jay Gatsby in **The Great Gatsby**? Gatsby's obsession with details— parties, flowers, invitations, the green light—was the stuff of legends. But imagine if he had AI to automate all this. Instead of obsessing over to-do lists, Gatsby could have spent more time nurturing the relationships he cared about most. Solo entrepreneurs, don't let the drudgery of logistics distract you from your own "green light"—the long-term vision your business is pursuing.

3. Prioritization Systems: The Pareto Principle on Steroids

The 80/20 rule, or Pareto Principle, tells us that 80% of results come from 20% of efforts. AI makes identifying that 20% easier than ever, whether through tools like **RescueTime**, which shows you exactly where your hours are being spent, or by integrating ChatGPT-like assistants into your workflow.

Imagine this scenario: instead of manually prioritizing emails or evaluating which client to focus on first, you use an AI tool to score your daily tasks based on effort versus revenue potential. One real-life solo entrepreneur I interviewed used this method to discover that a side project she'd been ignoring—a YouTube channel— actually had the highest engagement-to-sales conversion rate for her digital product. She shifted her priorities accordingly, resulting in a 40% increase in sales over six months—and, ironically, fewer hours spent chasing low-yield tasks.

Case Study: The Hyper-Productive Solopreneur

Let's analyze how one person integrated all these tools for maximum impact. Meet Jordan, a web developer based in Austin, Texas. Fresh out of a corporate job, Jordan wanted to focus on freelancing to earn more income and spend more time with his family. But his first six months out of the office looked a lot like his corporate hustle: 60-hour workweeks, inefficiency, and chronic overwhelm.

Then Jordan changed his approach.

- He adopted **Motion** for dynamic scheduling, ensuring his day wasn't derailed by interruptions.
- He used **Otter.ai** to transcribe client conversations in real-time, letting him free up afternoons for uninterrupted design sprints.
- Employing **Notion AI**, he automated weekly goal-setting sessions to highlight progress over busywork.
- Lastly, through RescueTime analytics, he realized that his time spent in Slack conversations—mostly small-talk with colleagues—was eroding 20% of his workday. He replaced Slack with streamlined client updates using Loom videos, saving him countless hours.

Jordan's income skyrocketed from $75,000 in Year 1 to over $190,000 by Year 3—all while working fewer hours. By leveraging AI, Jordan reclaimed his time without compromising quality or client satisfaction.

The Big Questions: What's Your Relationship with Time?

Now let me flip this conversation to you. Where is your time going, really? Are you a victim of burnout but hesitant to give up control? Have you resigned yourself to believing there are simply not enough hours in the day? These are uncomfortable questions, but they hold the key to your growth as a solo entrepreneur.

Here is your challenge: audit how you spend your time over the next week. Use a tool like RescueTime or Clockify to get a forensic-level understanding. Then ask yourself:

- How many of these tasks could be automated?
- Am I focusing on what drives the most impact? Or am I stuck in the weeds of "busy work"?
- If I had an entire day tomorrow for uninterrupted work, what would I accomplish?

Once you've answered these questions, put the AI tools we've discussed into action. Time management is less about squeezing more into your calendar and more about making room for what truly matters. What AI offers isn't simply optimization—it's freedom.

AI isn't here to take away your creativity, ambition, or work ethic. It's here to augment them. Like Gatsby gazing at his dream across the water, your big vision is waiting for you. The question is: are you brave enough to let go of the old ways and embrace the tools that will help you reach it faster?

The clock is ticking.

CHAPTER 10

PERSONAL BRANDING 2.0 WITH AI

I n the swells of the 21st century's digital tide, we no longer live in a world where mediocrity blends into the wallpaper. The attention economy demands not just competence but personality, commitment, and—most of all—a recognizable **brand**. Personal branding isn't a vanity project or an indulgence reserved for aspirational influencers; it's become a non-negotiable for anyone hoping to stand out in a world deafened by the cacophony of constant content. Whether you're an entrepreneur, a solopreneur, or a corporate maverick, your personal brand is as essential as your resume once was.

And just as tools like Microsoft Word transformed our resumes, artificial intelligence (AI) is here to supercharge your personal branding efforts. This is not just Personal Branding 1.0—it's 2.0, a hybrid of human creativity and machine intelligence. In this chapter, we'll explore how AI can help you craft, refine, and amplify your personal brand unlike ever before. But let's set the stage with this question: **If everything you've built suddenly disappeared overnight, would your personal brand be strong enough to resurrect it?**

The Evolution of Personal Branding: From Soap Boxes to Cyber Algorithms

To understand how AI fits into personal branding, we must first grasp its ever-changing nature. Decades ago, personal branding was reserved for titans of industry and cultural icons. Think Oprah Winfrey dominating daytime TV, Steve Jobs on a keynote stage in his signature black turtleneck, or Dr. Martin Luther King Jr. painting a technicolor dream with words alone.

Fast forward to the social media era. Now, anyone can have a platform and cultivate a persona with a smartphone and 15 minutes of inspiration. In this economy, "attention" is the currency—but the rules of the game have changed yet again. The bar isn't just capturing attention anymore; it's sustaining it. It's about creating multidimensional ecosystems where your authenticity, expertise, and impact harmonize into a cohesive narrative. And here's the kicker: AI is no longer just a passive tool; it's an active collaborator.

AI in personal branding is like the green light at the end of F. Scott Fitzgerald's **The Great Gatsby**: an infinite possibility that blurs the lines between aspiration and reality. AI won't define who you are—but it **can** help amplify your truth in ways that were unimaginable just a decade ago.

Building the Foundations of Personal Branding 2.0

Step 1: Clarify Your "Why" Before You Automate

Before plugging your brand into AI tools, pause to reflect on your core mission and purpose—your personal **why**. If you're familiar with my work, you'll know the power of building everything around your "why." Knowing what you stand for creates the foundation upon which every tweet, LinkedIn post, and TikTok video must stand firm.

Let me give you an example: take Tom Bilyeu, co-founder of Quest Nutrition and founder of Impact Theory. His personal brand is a direct outgrowth of his "why"—to empower people to unlock their potential. Every video he releases, every podcast he hosts, every Instagram quote he shares has this unifying heartbeat at its core. Companies may pivot, algorithms may shift, but that unwavering foundation remains his lighthouse.

AI cannot tell you your "why"—that is a journey you must take yourself. But once you know it, AI becomes your megaphone. It can streamline what you share, where you share, and even how effectively your message resonates with others.

Harnessing AI-Powered Tools for Personal Branding

Step 2: AI-Driven Content Creation

AI tools like ChatGPT (this very text's birth tool), Jasper, or Writesonic have democratized content creation. No longer does a personal brand rely on a Shakespearean turn of phrase. AI does the heavy lifting of ideation, drafting, and refining, allowing **you** to focus on creativity, strategy, and storytelling.

Take Jane, a freelance graphic designer who wanted to expand her audience on LinkedIn but struggled with writing. She used an AI tool to generate content ideas, prompted it with questions to draft her posts, and edited them to sound authentically "her." Instead of spending hours laboring over posts, she distilled her thoughts while AI filled in the blanks. Her presence exploded; she began generating engagement—and, more importantly, inbound clients.

AI content tools act like a co-writer who never tires. They can help you:

- Outline thought-leadership blog posts or LinkedIn articles.
- Write email newsletters tailored to your audience.
- Turn video transcripts into essays.
- Subtly adapt your content style for shifting audiences.

But here's where the rubber meets the road: while AI can craft the scaffolding of your message, it cannot build your emotional blueprint. When you use AI, ask yourself: **Am I infusing this text with my truth? Or am I becoming a hollow echo of others?**

And remember: the tools don't have imagination. **That is your role.**

Step 3: AI for Design & Visual Consistency

If AI tools are your creative teammates, think of AI graphic design platforms like Canva, Adobe Firefly, and Lensa as your digital Picasso. Personal branding isn't just linguistic; the visual element is equally critical. Visual consistency builds trust. When people see your content, they shouldn't need to double-check whose page they're on. That kind of instant recognition—**oh, that's hers**—can separate you from the digital herd.

Here's an example: Influencer Gary Vaynerchuk. His video thumbnails, power quotes, and social snippets have a distinctive style that screams "Gary Vee" even without his face. AI tools can help everyone—not just marketing wunderkinds—achieve this same cohesion.

Canva's AI features let solopreneurs generate branded templates enriched with your logo, brand colors, and fonts. You can also use tools like Runway AI to produce creative assets—from animations to ad banners. Need a professional headshot but don't want to pay $500? An AI photo tool like HeadshotPro can simulate one for a fraction of the effort.

But remember: AI amplifies **your** brand—it cannot create one from scratch. If your brand is poorly defined, AI will only multiply the confusion. Always ask yourself: **What story am I telling visually, and is it aligned with my core mission?**

Distributing Content with Precision & Scale

Step 4: AI for Audience Insights & Content Distribution

Marshall McLuhan, one of the 20th century's great media theorists, coined the phrase: **The medium is the message**. In today's internet ecosystem, the platform is the bridge between you and your audience. But choosing the right platform isn't instinctive—it's strategic. AI-powered analytics offer real-time insights into where your audience lives and what makes them tick.

Consider social media scheduling tools like Buffer or Hootsuite. These platforms, infused with AI, don't just schedule your posts— they **optimize** them. AI can determine the best time to post based on projected engagement rates. Even better, tools like SocialBee help identify which types of content resonate most with your followers—video vs. text, testimonials vs. thought leadership, and more.

For deeper analysis, sentiment-tracking tools like Brandwatch or Sprout Social use AI to let you peek into your audience's psyche, uncovering emotional responses to your content. Not every piece lands as you'd hope, but with AI, you can adapt, tweak, and evolve in real time.

Case in point: Remember when Rihanna strategically used her personal brand as the front window for her beauty empire, Fenty Beauty? Before launching her viral campaigns, she paid close attention to initial audience data to ensure inclusivity wasn't just a buzzword—it was her differentiator. AI allows you to translate such insights into actionable steps, ensuring your efforts remain audience-centric and impact-driven.

AI as Amplifier, Not Replacement

While the possibilities with AI are endless, I am reminded of a key lesson from American literary classics: any shortcut that removes the soul of the journey risks becoming **The Devil's Bargain**. Just like Faust in **Faustian legend**, automation without reflection tempts us into chasing the hollow metrics of likes, comments, and shares. Brand-building is a marathon, not a sprint.

Ask yourself: **When I look back on my personal branding journey, will I see a carefully curated image that only lived online—or a narrative so authentic, it carried me through the highs and lows of building my unicorn enterprise?**

You want AI to help tell your story—not overshadow it. Ensure each post, each campaign, and each strategy remains an extension of you. AI is the wind filling your sails, but the course? That's yours to chart.

Reflection: Your Brand, Your Responsibility

The marriage of personal branding and AI is a call to **rise above the noise.** AI is there to sharpen your tools, light your way, and deliver results at scale—but it's not there to pave over your responsibility to show up authentically. Ask yourself these two final questions:

1. If a stranger browsed through my social media, would they understand my "why" immediately?
2. If my AI were to disappear tomorrow, would my personal brand still stand strong?

In this age of algorithms and automation, let your personal brand remain the one thing that cannot be manufactured. A brand born of purpose, amplified by AI, and sustained through trust? That, my friend, is your competitive edge.

Welcome to Personal Branding 2.0. The rest is up to you.

CHAPTER 11

CRACKING THE CODE
OF REVENUE STREAMS WITH AI

I n F. Scott Fitzgerald's **The Great Gatsby**, there's a recurring image of a green light, gleaming across the bay, just out of reach but always present. For solo entrepreneurs, the green light often represents financial independence—a life of freedom, creativity, and impact, supported by stable revenue streams that don't ebb and flow with every market hiccup. But how do you take that shimmering ideal, seemingly distant, and make it a reality you can touch? How do you transcend the feast-and-famine cycle so many small business owners endure and create not just one, but multiple revenue streams—diverse, scalable, and sustainable?

The answer: artificial intelligence.

Think of AI not as some cold, impersonal disruptor, but as the golden key that unlocks doors to revenue models you may never have considered. In this chapter, we'll dive deep into **how** AI can help you architect and scale multiple income streams, even if you're a solo entrepreneur with limited resources or technical skills. We'll focus on practical, actionable strategies, using real-world examples and a step-by-step breakdown of how to make it all work. Along the way, I'll ask you to challenge some of your own assumptions about how revenue can (and should) flow into your business. Because, as Fitzgerald reminds us, the future we're striving for often demands that we let go of the past.

The Mindset Shift: From Linear Income to Dynamic Flows

Before we dive into the nuts and bolts of AI-powered revenue streams, let's address something critical: your relationship with money. Most entrepreneurs start out chasing **linear income**. They trade their time and expertise for dollars—consulting gigs, coaching sessions, or freelance projects. It feels tangible, predictable, and safe at first. But here's the problem: linear income is a trap. Your energy and attention are finite, so your earning potential always has a ceiling.

What's needed is a mindset shift—to stop thinking in one dimension and start thinking in dynamic flows, much like the interconnected rivers of the Mississippi Delta. AI is the tributary that feeds these rivers, making it possible to earn money in your sleep, scale without equivalent effort, and diversify your risk. If this sounds pie-in-the-sky, I hear you. But hang in there—by the end of this chapter, you'll see just how attainable this is.

Revenue Stream #1: AI-Powered Subscription Models

Imagine this: You're a seasoned mindfulness coach with a library of guided meditations sitting on Google Drive. They're good, your clients love them, but they're underutilized. Now imagine turning these meditations into a subscription-based app powered by AI.

Let's take it step by step:

1. **Start with Personalization:** AI excels at customizing experiences. Using basic machine learning models, you can create a simple app that tracks user preferences—length of meditations, themes (stress relief, focus, sleep)—and recommends content tailored to their needs. The more they interact with the app, the more it learns about them, continuously refining its suggestions.

2. **Automate Engagement:** Use conversational AI (like ChatGPT) to enhance user experience. For example, you can integrate a chatbot

that checks in on users, provides motivational nudges, or suggests uplifting content when their activity dips.

3. **Low-Code, No-Code Tools:** Building an app no longer requires a degree in computer science. Platforms like Bubble, Adalo, or Glide can help you design your product with minimal technical skills. Add an AI personalization engine like ChatGPT or Firebase ML for behavior-based analytics, and suddenly, you have a product.

4. **Recurring Revenue:** By charging a modest monthly subscription fee—even $7.99—you can build a predictable revenue stream that grows exponentially as your audience scales.

Case Study: Calm, the mindfulness app, is valued at over $2 billion, and while their team is massive now, their roots were scrappy. They launched with a handful of recorded meditations and basic AI algorithms. Solo entrepreneurs can replicate this model on a smaller scale, filling niche markets—mindfulness for parents, creative professionals, or entrepreneurs—and compete by being hyper-specific.

Challenge for You: What unique knowledge or content do you have that could be transformed into a subscription model? How could AI personalize the user journey to make your offer indispensable?

Revenue Stream #2: AI-Trained SaaS Products

Software-as-a-service (SaaS) is a tech-heavy term that intimidates many non-tech entrepreneurs. But let's demystify it: SaaS is simply software that solves a recurring problem and gets delivered to users online. And thanks to AI, it's more accessible than ever to build a SaaS product as a solo founder.

Three Elements of AI-Powered SaaS Success

1. **Find the Pain Point:** Start with a specific, well-defined problem. For example, let's say you're a freelance copywriter. You know that small businesses struggle to generate effective email marketing campaigns. That's your pain point.

2. **Leverage AI for the Heavy Lifting:** Using platforms like OpenAI, Hugging Face, or Google AutoML, you can train an AI model to

generate tailored email sequences for different industries. Layer in Natual Language Processing (NLP) to analyze successful campaigns and continuously optimize outputs.

3. **Keep it Simple:** Many successful SaaS products thrive because they do one thing extremely well. Don't try to build the next Salesforce; it's too broad. Instead, focus narrowly. Your AI-powered email sequence generator could be marketed as "Email Genie," delivering pre-written campaigns in under 10 seconds.

Done Is Better Than Perfect

Here's a myth I want to debunk right now: You don't need to build the Mona Lisa of SaaS products from Day 1. The founder of Buffer (a social media scheduling tool) launched his product with just a landing page and a PayPal button to see if people would sign up. Validate your idea, build lean, and iterate over time.

Case Study: Copy.ai began as a solo founder's idea: to create AI tools for writing marketing copy. By leveraging OpenAI GPT models and starting with a bare-bones MVP, they rapidly attracted paying subscribers. Today, they're generating millions in annual revenue with a small team.

Challenge for You: What's one recurring problem you (or your clients) deal with that could be solved by software? How could AI automate or enhance the solution?

Revenue Stream #3: Affiliate and Partnership Models Supercharged by AI

Affiliate marketing and brand partnerships have been around for decades, but AI can turbocharge the potential for income here.

Enhancing Affiliate Income with AI

Let's say you're an online fitness coach with an affiliate partnership with a nutrition brand. Instead of relying solely on generic blog posts or email blasts to promote products, you can harness AI:

- **Predictive Analytics:** AI models like Google Looker or Tableau can analyze customer behavior, making it easier to identify which segments of your audience are most likely to buy the products you recommend.
- **Dynamic Content Creation:** Use AI copywriting tools like Jasper to create personalized product recommendations for each customer based on their fitness goals, dietary preferences, and past purchases.
- **Chatbot Sales Assistants:** Deploy a conversational AI chatbot (think of it as your virtual sales rep) on your website to guide customers seamlessly toward affiliate purchases.

Case Study: AI-Powered Influencers

Consider the rise of virtual influencers like Lil Miquela—an entirely AI-generated online personality with millions of followers. While this might feel futuristic, the principle is clear: AI allows you to scale your influence and partnership opportunities far beyond what a single person could manually achieve.

Challenge for You: Who in your network could benefit from an AI-enhanced affiliate marketing strategy? What partnerships or products align with your expertise that you could start promoting right away?

Revenue Stream #4: AI-Enhanced Digital Products

Digital products—online courses, templates, e-books—might not sound revolutionary. But AI can take them to the next level, making them more valuable and profitable.

Example: Adaptive Courses

Let's say you're a graphic designer creating an online course on Canva design basics. Using AI, you could implement adaptive learning—a technique where the course content adjusts in real time based on a learner's progress. Struggling with typography? The next module would automatically include extra practice exercises on fonts. Setting up something like this a decade ago would've required huge budgets and intricate programming, but tools like Teachable and LearnDash now allow seamless AI integration.

Dynamic Templates and Tools

Another option is creating dynamic, AI-enhanced templates for businesses. For instance:

- Marketing strategy templates that use AI to auto-fill based on industry trends.
- Financial planning spreadsheets with built-in AI to forecast cash flow.

Case Study: Canva recently integrated AI tools like Magic Write, where users can generate entire social media posts or presentations in seconds. Start thinking about how **you** can build simple digital tools that your audience will love.

Challenge for You: How can AI turn your static digital products into dynamic tools that grow in value the more people use them?

Pulling It All Together

Building AI-powered revenue streams isn't just about leveraging technology; it's about thinking like a systems architect. Each of these streams—subscriptions, SaaS products, affiliate partnerships, and digital tools—can feed into one another, creating a robust ecosystem of income. For instance, your SaaS product might promote your digital courses, which, in turn, drive affiliate sales—all while each stream runs largely on autopilot thanks to AI.

Your Next Step

Here's my question to you: What's stopping you from building multiple streams of revenue today? Is it fear of technology? A belief that it's too complicated? Because I promise you, it's not. Tools like ChatGPT, AutoML, and no-code platforms are designed to make AI accessible—even to those without a tech background.

Remember that green light across the bay. It may feel out of reach now, but it isn't. With AI as your compass, it's closer than you think. So take a deep breath, start small, and step into the future of entrepreneurship. This time, the green light isn't a dream—it's your destination.

CHAPTER 12

BUILDING EXCEPTIONAL CUSTOMER EXPERIENCES

"It is not true that we have only one life to live; if we can read, we can live as many more lives and as many kinds of lives as we wish."

— S.I. Hayakawa.

This insight from Hayakawa could just as easily be applied to your customers. Every interaction they have with your business is a chance to live a story—a story you're crafting with them, not for them. The best businesses today engage in storytelling at scale, making each customer feel as though they're the protagonist of a tailor-made narrative. This chapter will show you how to build unforgettable customer experiences— experiences that drive loyalty, advocacy, and sustainable success—using the power of data, artificial intelligence (AI), and, more importantly, empathy.

Why Customer Experience is the Foundation of Success

Imagine walking into a small-town bookstore, the kind immortalized in novels like **The Storied Life of A.J. Fikry** by Gabrielle Zevin. The smell of old paper lingers in the air; the owner greets you by name, remembers that quirky poetry collection you picked up last year, and suggests a new book that aligns perfectly with your taste. How does that make you feel? Understood? Seen? Special?

Now, imagine walking into a chain bookstore where the cashier doesn't look up, the titles feel generic, and you're directed to a self-checkout kiosk when you need a recommendation. Both stores sell books. But one leaves you with an experience you'll remember and share, while the other fades into the forgettable blur of mediocrity.

This is the essence of customer experience. It's not about transactions—it's about connections. And while the analog charm of the neighborhood bookstore is hard to replicate in a digital-first world, it's far from impossible. Thanks to AI, data analytics, and intentionally crafted touchpoints, we can now scale that intimate, bespoke experience, multiplying it across thousands—even millions—of customers.

But here's the hard truth: customer experience is not a department. It's not a chatbot. And it's not just a gimmicky rewards program. It's your entire business. Creating exceptional customer experiences doesn't require the biggest budget or the trendiest tech—it requires an obsession with understanding your customer and meeting them where they are.

Are you truly listening to your customers? Are you willing to rethink every element of your business through the lens of their journey? And most importantly—if not you, then who?

The Marriage of AI and Empathy: A Winning Formula

For many entrepreneurs, AI still feels like the wizard in **The Wonderful Wizard of Oz**—mysterious, vaguely magical, and maybe a little menacing. But AI isn't some distant sorcery—it's your customer's most sophisticated ally.

Here's an example: Netflix. It sounds like old hat to hail Netflix as a pinnacle of customer experience, but their algorithms consistently recommend shows and movies with uncanny precision. Their AI "remembers" us at a scale that no human could. Yet here's the kicker: Netflix's personalization isn't just about tech. You'll notice their interface is simple, inviting, and conversational. Their copywriting, their custom graphics, their human-curated "Top 10"—these elements add the human touch the AI system cannot. They marry cold computing power with warm empathy.

Netflix begins where most businesses fail: they **choose** to know their customers. They've invested resources into understanding the behaviors, preferences, and consumption patterns of millions. And this obsession isn't history class—it's happening in real time.

Now, stop and ask yourself: What data are you collecting about your customers? What story does that data tell you? And most importantly, how are you acting on it? Even as a small business, you generate data at every stage of the customer journey. Are you capturing it? Are you leveraging it to draw closer to your next sale—or further away?

Every business today has access to AI. Tools like HubSpot, Salesforce, and ChatGPT have democratized advanced data analytics and customer understanding. But having access to these tools isn't enough; it's what you **do** with the insights AI provides that counts.

Take Amazon, for example. Their AI tracks not just what you buy, but what you browse, compare, and abandon in your cart. From this information, Amazon crafts an experience: reminders of forgotten items, sudden price drops, personalized email campaigns, and preemptive instructions on products you haven't even purchased yet. Amazon's ethos isn't just about being "Earth's most customer-centric company"—it's about making the customer feel like the universe orbits around them.

Does your business have that level of clarity? If your customer shopkeeper—the AI assistant—were standing in front of you wearing a tweed blazer, what would they have to say about your customers? Would they know their favorite color? Their frustration? Their aspirations? If this metaphorical "AI assistant" is a silent presence in the corner of the room, unused and undervalued, you're leaving legacy-defining opportunities on the table.

Hyper-Personalization: Treating Your Customers Like Snowflakes

Slot machines have one job: they pull people in. Through flashing lights, slot games exploit randomness and micro-rewards, creating individualized experiences within a crowded casino. Slots are personalized, even if in a subtle, manipulative way. Customer experience can be similar—but with integrity.

Hyper-personalization takes this concept and infuses it with precision and intent. Instead of just clustering customers into groups (e.g., "millennials," "moms," "sports fans"), hyper-personalization uses AI to deliver experiences to specific individuals. Imagine sending a customer an email that doesn't just say, "Here's what's new," but instead says, "Hey Carlos, based on that bamboo chair you were researching last week, we think you'll **love** this new collection of sustainable office furniture."

A real-world hyper-personalization champion is Spotify. Their "Wrapped" campaign is an annual masterstroke. People share their Wrapped playlists like badges of honor on social media, because Spotify uses their own listening data to tell them something they may not have even realized: their story. It's genius branding, but it's also a pinnacle of customer experience. Spotify doesn't just say, "Here's what you listened to." It narrates a relationship between you and your music that feels deep, meaningful, and proprietary. Your Wrapped is your personal fingerprint.

What fingerprint are you giving your customers? How are you showing them that your product or service is tailored just for them? Modern customers expect—no, demand—this level of recognition, even from businesses just starting out. The technology exists—it's up to you to wield it.

Case Study: Warby Parker and the Power of Convenient Empathy

Warby Parker isn't a tech company by definition, but their customer experience is a case study in using digital tools to reimagine brick-and-mortar industries. Founded in 2010, they asked a provocative question: Why does buying glasses feel like getting your passport renewed at the DMV?

Warby Parker cracked the code by using technology to deliver empathy. Their "Home Try-on" program disrupted the eyewear industry by allowing customers to order five pairs of glasses, try them on at home, and return the ones they didn't like. Warby Parker used AI and a slick UX to simplify what had become a cumbersome, frustrating process.

But they didn't stop there. Using facial recognition technology, Warby Parker's app allows potential buyers to **virtually** try on frames, removing yet another barrier to purchase. Yet behind these tools, there's always a beating heart. If you opt to visit one of their stores, you'll find friendly staff trained to mirror the simplicity of their online experience. They meet each customer on their terms—whether online or in-store—and that's the secret sauce.

Think now: Where is your Warby Parker moment? Where can you combine high-tech solutions with radically low-friction empathy? If you don't make your customer's life noticeably better, what's motivating their loyalty?

Turning Friction into Fuel

The author James Baldwin once said, "Not everything that is faced can be changed, but nothing can be changed until it is faced." He wasn't talking about business, but he might as well have been.

Every company has friction points in its customer experience. The checkout process might be clunky, the chatbot confusing, the return policy restrictive, or the follow-up email absent. These are the equivalent of rocks in your customers' shoes. Small, but deeply annoying.

Here's your challenge: find your friction points. Talk to your customers. Read your reviews. Walk through the sales process yourself, as a mystery shopper might. Be brutally honest with yourself. Then, use artificial intelligence to reduce or eliminate those friction points.

Tesla, for all its controversies, approaches this brilliantly. Their purchasing process for a vehicle is seamless. Unlike traditional car dealerships, you can buy a Tesla entirely online in under 15 minutes. No pushy salespeople, no haggling, no confusion—just a Netflix-like simplicity that feels intuitive and self-powered. Every step of the transaction is clear, direct, and customer-centric.

So: where in your business can you cut complexity? Can you deliver magic instead of mediocrity?

Looking Forward: Build with the Heart of a Small Business, the Spirit of a Giant

The iconic poet Walt Whitman wrote, **"I am large, I contain multitudes."** It's the ideal ethos for the modern business. Even as you grow, integrating AI and automations, never lose sight of why you started: to solve a problem, to meet a need, to leave your customers happier than you found them.

AI won't do the work for you, but it will empower your vision. Think of AI as your Watson, not your Sherlock Holmes; a partner who amplifies your humanity rather than replaces it. Your job is to use these tools to build a business that feels like that neighborhood bookstore—personal, warm, unforgettable—at a scale your younger self couldn't have dreamed of.

To close, I'll leave you with this question: What will your customers remember about your business? Use AI to make the answer unforgettable.

CHAPTER 13

CREATING CONTENT
AT SCALE WITH GENERATIVE AI

In the early pages of F. Scott Fitzgerald's **The Great Gatsby**, Nick Carraway describes Gatsby's boundless ambition, likening him to a boat beating ceaselessly against the current. In many ways, building a business as a solo entrepreneur can feel the same: driven by dreams yet constantly battling the constraints of time, energy, and resources. Perhaps the most glaring of these constraints, especially in today's world, is keeping up with the sheer volume of content required to stay relevant, visible, and competitive. Content is the bridge between your business and your audience. It tells your story, cultivates trust, and plants seeds in hearts that grow into loyalty. But producing high-quality content at scale? For many, it's like pushing that boat against the tide with nothing but a wooden oar.

That's where generative AI steps in. If traditional content creation is rowing laboriously upstream, generative AI is the motor that propels you forward effortlessly. Tools like GPT, DALL·E, and Stable Diffusion allow you to create text, images, and multimedia at a scale that was once unthinkable for an individual entrepreneur. They turn what might have been an insurmountable bottleneck into a wellspring of opportunity.

In this chapter, we'll explore how generative AI can be used as a strategic lever to produce high-quality content at scale, diving into real-world examples, practical applications, and ethical considerations. Think of this chapter not as a tutorial, but as a roadmap. Where will you take it?

The Content Crunch: Why Scale Matters More Than Ever

Before we explore the "how," let's talk about the "why." Why does content at **scale** matter so much—not just any content, but consistently high-quality, high-value content?

Consider the entrepreneur who opens a bakery, hoping to differentiate herself with artisanal sourdough. Initially, word of mouth and a few Instagram posts are enough to attract neighbors. But over time, the audience plateaus. New customers don't stumble in. Competitors start siphoning away attention with more engaging social feeds, online recipes, and stories about their locally sourced practices. To thrive, she needs to expand her visibility—launching videos, blog posts, newsletters, Tweets (or X's), TikToks, and more. And not just once, but consistently. This requires content—a lot of it.

For solo entrepreneurs, the math of traditional content creation doesn't work. Writing blogs takes hours. Producing videos is resource-intensive. Social media micro-content demands persistent effort to churn out ideas, visuals, captions, and hashtags. The sheer workload can be overwhelming, leaving little room for actual business building. And yet, this content is the engine that drives everything: lead generation, customer loyalty, thought leadership.

This is the pivot point where generative AI becomes a game-changer: it's not just a tool; it's an **amplifier**. It's you—your ideas, your voice, your vision—multiplied.

The Machines as Coauthors: Working with Generative AI

One misconception that often keeps people from using generative AI is the assumption that it will replace them entirely—or worse, strip away the authenticity of their content. Let me clarify something: Generative AI does not replace the creator; it augments the creator.

Imagine AI as your creative partner, much like John Steinbeck described his notebooks during the writing of **East of Eden**: "a repository of thoughts, a place where ideas evolve." Tools like GPT act as that creative notebook, but one that also happens to write back—helping you brainstorm, draft, iterate, and polish in ways that make the process exponentially faster and richer.

Let's break this down, medium by medium.

1. Text at Scale: The GPT Wizardry

If you're like most entrepreneurs, you've already had those moments staring at a blank screen, wondering how to get started on your next blog post or newsletter. Think of GPT (Generative Pre-trained Transformer) as your personal ghostwriter, ready to throw ideas at the wall to jumpstart your creative process.

Use Case: A Solo Consultant's Blog Strategy

Meet Kevin, a solo business coach specializing in leadership development for small teams. His value proposition? Empathy-driven management. Kevin knows his audience loves actionable content paired with real-world examples. But writing articles every week is grueling.

Kevin uses GPT to streamline his process:

1. **Prompting Ideas:** He types a query like, "What are unique topics about empathetic leadership?" Within seconds, GPT offers a list: how empathy prevents burnout, using empathy to resolve team conflict, empathetic innovation, and so on.
2. **Drafting Faster:** Kevin picks one topic, "Empathy as a Burnout Shield." He inputs a detailed prompt to GPT, asking it to draft a 1,000-word blog post that features statistics, relatable case studies, and includes a counter-argument to keep the discussion dynamic.
3. **Iterating with AI:** Kevin reads the draft and tweaks it to fit his tone and voice—more conversational, less formal. He uses editing tools to refine flow and structure, cutting his time-to-publish from five hours to one.

The result? A scalable blog strategy that grows his traffic without growing his stress. GPT is not taking over Kevin's blog; it's helping him show up more consistently and effectively.

Challenge for You: What pieces of your content could currently use extra polish or speed to market? Could you let go of perfection and use AI for first drafts, then layer in your personal flair? Remember: rough diamonds can be polished; an empty screen cannot.

2. Visual Storytelling with DALL·E and Stable Diffusion

In today's visual-first world, images are non-negotiable. A picture on social media can convey emotion and magnetize attention in milliseconds. But creating custom visuals? That's an entirely different headache—unless you have a creative team or happen to double as a graphic designer. Enter tools like DALL·E and Stable Diffusion, which generate stunning, custom images based on written prompts.

Use Case: Marketing for a Novelty Product

Imagine Sara, a solo founder of a novelty sock company. Each sock design is unique—quirky patterns inspired by pop culture and current events. To grow her brand, Sara wants to create an ongoing series of Instagram graphics and story reels that showcase her socks in imaginative, dreamlike scenarios. Hiring a designer for every post would drain her bootstrap budget.

Instead, Sara leans on DALL·E:

1. **Creative Inputs:** Sara prompts DALL·E with ideas like, "A whimsical cityscape made entirely of socks," or "A pair of socks styled as astronauts, floating on the surface of the moon."
2. **Iterative Refinement:** She generates dozens of images in minutes and selects her top-tier creations. She sometimes tweaks her prompts to get variations or slightly different aesthetics.

3. **Compositing and Branding:** Once she has the raw images, Sara enhances them within Canva, adding her logo, product descriptions, and captions.

What once felt like an impossible task—out-creating bigger brands with deeper marketing budgets—now feels achievable. DALL·E became her virtual visual designer, expanding her creative bandwidth without expanding her costs.

Challenge for You: Next time you think, "I wish I had a better image for this," give yourself permission to experiment with generative art tools. What might your product, service, or brand look like in a universe far bigger than static stock photos?

3. Video and Multimedia Content: The Next Frontier

While tools like GPT aid in text, and DALL·E sparks graphics, what if your ambition goes further? What if you want to produce entire videos, presentations, or multimedia campaigns without the need for videographers and editors at every step? Emerging AI tools like Runway ML and Pictory are paving the way.

Example: A Course Creator in Overload

Meet Jamie, an online educator building courses on mindful productivity techniques. Jamie knows video is king when it comes to remote learning, but creating polished course videos with compelling visuals, animations, and captions is a herculean effort.

Here's how Jamie incorporates AI into the workflow:

1. **Scriptwriting:** GPT helps outline course scripts and even adds summaries, key learning points, and metaphors to make concepts click.
2. **Image and Animation:** Jamie uses tools like Runway ML to create simple animations or interactive visuals without needing an animator.
3. **Video Editing Automation:** Instead of learning advanced editing software, Jamie uses Pictory to automate tasks like caption generation, background music integration, and visual overlays.

The result is a cohesive, professional video-based course—built not by a massive studio team, but by a single entrepreneur leveraging AI.

Challenge for You: What multimedia formats (video, presentations, podcasts) could elevate your connection with your audience? How might automation overcome your hesitations?

Ethical Considerations: The Soul of Your Content

Before we conclude, let's touch on the elephant in the room: ethics. While generative AI makes creating content easy, the **right way** to use it matters. Content produced mindlessly—or worse, used to mislead—has the potential to deteriorate trust.

Think of your audience as readers of **To Kill a Mockingbird**. They see through insincerity as clearly as Scout Finch sees through the hypocrisy of her small-town neighbors. AI should be your ally, not your mask. Always maintain creative ownership and transparency. Acknowledge when you've used AI and, more importantly, infuse your human perspective into what you produce.

The Call to Action: Scale with Intention

Generative AI is not a magic shortcut. It's an engine—but you are the pilot. Scaling content is only valuable if it deepens your impact, sharpens your messaging, and strengthens your connection with those you serve. As you explore these tools, ask yourself: What do I want to create? Who do I want to serve? How can I scale without losing sight of my why?

One of my favorite moments from American literature comes from Steinbeck's **Of Mice and Men**, when George reminds Lennie of their shared dream: "We got a future. We got somebody to talk to that gives a damn about us." As a solo entrepreneur, that's what your content should give to your audience: a sense of connection, community, and belief that someone understands **their** journey.

The tools are now in your hands to do so—not slower, but at scale.

CHAPTER 14

ETHICAL AI: NAVIGATING THE RISKS AND RESPONSIBILITIES

n **The Great Gatsby**, F. Scott Fitzgerald invites us into the opulent world of Jay Gatsby, a man who builds his empire on dreams, ambition, and—let's not mince words—moral ambiguity. At first, the grandeur of his vision seems intoxicating, intoxicating enough to make us complicit in a way. Yet as the story unfolds, the cracks in Gatsby's foundation reveal themselves: the shortcuts he's taken, the corners he's cut, the lives—literally and figuratively—he's destroyed. In many ways, modern entrepreneurs venturing into the realm of artificial intelligence are facing their own Gatsby moment. The power of AI holds tremendous promise, yet without clear ethical boundaries, that same power can result in devastating consequences.

The question we must ask ourselves in this chapter is: **What kind of Gatsbys do we want to be?** Are we willing to compromise morality for perceived greatness, or can we build empires grounded in accountability, fairness, and, above all, humanity? This chapter isn't just a philosophical inquiry—it's a practical guide to help you, the entrepreneur, navigate the risks of bias, misinformation, and privacy violations that come with wielding AI. If you're planning to use AI to create the next disruptive unicorn business, you'll need more than cutting-edge algorithms. You'll need principles. You'll need ethics. Let's dig in.

The Invisible Hand: How Bias Creeps Into AI

When most of us think of bias, we think of human prejudice—the kind of stereotyping or discrimination we've been trying to chip away at for centuries. But bias in AI is far more subtle, far more insidious, and in many cases, far more damaging. To put it bluntly, algorithms aren't born into the world unbiased. They inherit the values, assumptions, and limitations of their creators. They reflect the data they're fed, much like children absorbing the beliefs and behaviors of their parents. And just as children can grow up mirroring the prejudices of their environment, AI inherits the biases of the datasets it consumes.

Take, for example, the infamous case of COMPAS, an AI tool used in the U.S. judicial system to predict the likelihood of criminal recidivism. A 2016 investigation by ProPublica found that the tool was significantly more likely to label Black defendants as "high risk" compared to white defendants, even when controlling for factors like the nature of the crime and prior history. The issue wasn't that the algorithm was overtly "racist," but rather that its training data reflected societal inequalities, making it a mirror to the existing biases in our justice system.

Here's the challenge for entrepreneurs: if your product or service relies on data to make decisions, what invisible biases might you be unintentionally inheriting? Whether you're building an AI-driven HR platform to streamline hiring or launching a retail app that uses machine learning to suggest products, the datasets you rely on will encode historical inequities unless you actively work to mitigate them. Bias isn't just an ethical liability—it's a business risk. An AI that discriminates or fails segments of your user base might not be uncovered immediately, but trust me, it **will** be uncovered. And in a hyper-transparent digital era, a loss of trust like that can cripple your unicorn prospects overnight.

Actionable Framework #1: Bias Audits

To counteract bias, conduct regular "bias audits" of your AI model. Just like the corporate world conducts financial audits to ensure accountability, you need to create a system that consistently reviews your algorithm for unintended biases. Questions to ask in your bias audit include:

1. Who is represented in my dataset? Who isn't?

If your data doesn't reflect the diversity of your customer base, it's a problem. Imagine building an AI-driven beauty platform that recommends products based on skin tone—but only trained on images of light-skinned individuals. The backlash would be swift and deserved (just ask certain makeup brands that have faced similar criticisms).

2. What outcomes am I optimizing for, and are those outcomes equitable?

Profit-driven metrics are fine, but they shouldn't come at the cost of fairness. Consider re-weighting your model to account for societal inequities. If you're designing an AI for hiring, for instance, you might choose to remove certain proxies from your dataset that historically correlate with class, gender, or race.

3. Who is evaluating this system?

Diverse teams create better outcomes. If your technical team doesn't include voices from varied backgrounds, you're increasing the likelihood of blind spots.

The Post-Truth Epidemic: Misinformation and the AI Arms Race

If bias is the AI entrepreneur's shadowy reflection, then misinformation is its trick mirror—a distortion that can feel deceptive and destabilizing. AI-driven misinformation is running rampant across every sector, from media to advertising to politics. Generative AI tools, like deepfake video creators or text generators, can fabricate entire universes of false narratives with jaw-dropping realism.

Here's an example that should make every entrepreneur shiver: In 2023, a deepfake video of a well-known CEO announcing a fake mass layoff went viral across social media. Although the misinformation was debunked within 24 hours, the company's stock price plunged by nearly 8%, erasing billions in market value.

Consider, for a moment, the scale of responsibility you hold if your AI product could be weaponized to spread falsehoods. Even if that's not your **intended** use case, unintended misuse can still cause irrevocable harm. If you've ever found yourself wondering, "But how could someone use my platform for evil?", it's already too late.

Actionable Framework #2: Guardrails for Truth

How do you safeguard against your AI becoming a vessel for misinformation? Start by building what I call "guardrails for truth":

1. Transparency in your algorithms.

Make it clear how your AI works. For example, if your platform uses AI-generated recommendations, include disclaimers so users know the role automation plays. The more opaque your systems, the easier they are to manipulate.

2. Validation protocols.

Establish rigorous checks for accuracy. Wikipedia, while not perfect, became a global knowledge repository by building a consensus model where inaccuracies are corrected in near real-time. What systems can you build into your product to allow users—or other experts—to flag and correct mistakes?

3. Proactive misuse testing.

Consult with fraud experts, cybersecurity professionals, and ethicists as part of your development process. Hack your own product in-house before it launches; think like the bad actors so you can stay two steps ahead.

Whose Secrets Are Safe? The Crisis of AI and Privacy

Privacy violations may be the most personal of AI's risks, but they are no less significant in terms of scale. Think of every piece of personal data we generate daily: our search histories, GPS locations, purchase preferences, even the way we scroll. Now imagine an AI system indiscriminately collecting, analyzing, and selling that information without the user's informed consent.

A recent case that rattled Silicon Valley involved a fitness app that inadvertently exposed the locations of military bases simply because it tracked user jogging routes via GPS. The app's creators likely had no malicious intent, but the lack of robust safeguards turned its customers—who just wanted fitness insights—into unwitting participants in a significant security breach.

As entrepreneurs stepping into AI, the question isn't just **how much data can we collect**, but **how much data should we collect?**

Actionable Framework #3: Privacy-First Design

To safeguard user privacy, implement a privacy-first design philosophy:

1. Minimize what you collect.

The less data you store, the lower the chances of misuse. For example, consider anonymizing datasets or implementing on-device processing where sensitive information doesn't have to be sent to central servers.

2. Be radically transparent.

Create privacy policies that are written in plain English (or your target audience's language), not legalese. Facebook once lost the trust of millions because users didn't fully understand how their data was being used. Clarity matters.

3. Empower user control.

Your customers should dictate what gets shared and when. Build robust opt-out systems that go beyond just checking a tiny box in a form.

4. Prepare for breaches.

Have protocols in place to immediately handle data breaches. If you wait until a breach happens to figure out how to respond, you're already too late. Own the narrative by being proactive.

The Soul of Your Unicorn

As we close this chapter, I want to leave you with a question—one that forces you to look in the mirror as you shape your AI venture: **Where does your responsibility begin, and where does it end?**

Entrepreneurs often think of themselves as disruptors, dreamers, the ones who see the world differently. That's your superpower. But as you harness AI, remember that disruption without accountability is just destruction. Building a unicorn isn't just about scaling fast; it's about scaling ethically. It's about leaving the world better than you found it.

AI is a tool, no more inherently good or evil than a hammer or a paintbrush. What matters is the intention and care with which it's wielded. If we're going to build empires worth remembering, we need to combine ambition not just with grit, but with integrity. You may or may not think of yourself as a modern-day Jay Gatsby. Even so, ask: when the history books (or the startups) write about you, will your story inspire admiration or cautionary tales?

That choice—entirely, unequivocally—is yours.

CHAPTER 15

FUNDRAISING AS
A SOLO AI ENTREPRENEUR

I n Margaret Mitchell's **Gone with the Wind**, Scarlett O'Hara famously declares, "I'll never be hungry again," embodying both desperation and resolve. For many solo AI entrepreneurs, fundraising can feel like Scarlett's moment—an act born out of necessity, rooted in fierce determination to thrive. Like Scarlett, you stand in your fields of possibility, facing what might feel like a daunting battle to secure your future. But what you may not realize is that today, you're wielding an unfair advantage—your AI venture.

The AI factor transforms fundraising from a Sisyphean upward climb into something more akin to Gatsby's green light—a tantalizing opportunity on the horizon, drawing investors toward the promise of abundant, scalable innovation. But how do you harness this advantage? How do you attract capital while working solo? How do you build trust in a vision that only you carry? And most importantly, how do you do all this without losing your soul—or your ownership—in the process?

This chapter answers these questions and equips you with the strategies, mindset, and anecdotes to secure the funding you need without compromising the independence and ingenuity that make your solo venture so uniquely powerful.

Pitching to VCs: Selling the Dream, Not Just the Code

Whether you love them or loathe them, venture capitalists (VCs) are often the gatekeepers of scalable funding. But if you're a solo entrepreneur, you're already swimming upstream. VCs are used to funding teams, not a single individual. Many will (unfairly) question your capacity to execute alone or your long-term resilience. Herein lies your first challenge: how do you sell the dream when you're the only one steering the ship?

The key lies in creating a magnetic narrative around your AI venture that shifts attention away from your solo status and toward the transformational potential of your product. Remember, VCs aren't investing in **you**—they're investing in the scalable promise of your idea, the market opportunity, and your ability to execute.

Take the story of Pieter Levels, the solo entrepreneur behind **Nomad List**. While not an AI business, Levels built Nomad List as a one-man operation and bootstrapped it to $500,000 in annual revenue without taking VC funding. But imagine if Levels had walked into a VC meeting with just his vision—a massive global network for digital nomads—accentuated by data-driven insights from machine learning or AI systems. His pitch would be unstoppable. Why? Because he could have simultaneously highlighted the market's untapped demand and positioned himself as the sole visionary who could deliver an AI-powered solution.

When pitching to VCs, your framework is simple but effective:

1. The "Why Now?" Hook

Why is this the opportune moment for your AI-driven solution to emerge? Tie your venture to emerging trends—whether it's the rise of generative AI, the explosion of edge computing, or regulatory shifts in industries like healthcare or finance. Timing is everything to a VC. A great example is Jasper AI, an AI-driven content creation tool that capitalized beautifully on the growing demand for automated copywriting in digital marketing. Jasper didn't just solve a problem; they solved it at the right moment.

2. Make the AI Factor Shine

Investors know the buzzwords—machine learning, generative AI, large language models. They're not impressed by jargon, but they ARE mesmerized by clear, clean use cases where AI creates compounding value. Show your prototype. Run a live demonstration. If you're building an AI-powered SaaS tool, show how the AI improves exponentially over time with more user data. If your AI learns, adapts, and creates unique insights, you're articulating a defensible moat—exactly what VCs love to hear.

3. Address the "Solo Founder" Elephant in the Room

The solo-founder bias in the VC world is real. To counteract it, lean into your strengths. You can move faster and iterate more rapidly than a team. You're not bogged down by decision-making gridlocks. Build personal credibility by highlighting past projects you've successfully executed on your own. Position yourself as a modern-day Ishmael from **Moby-Dick**—not just surviving your solitary voyage, but thriving because of it.

The Crowdfunding Angle: Build a Movement, Not Just a Product

Crowdfunding has become the **Walden Pond** of entrepreneurship—free from traditional constraints, a space for independent thinkers to attract grassroots support. And for solo AI entrepreneurs, it's fertile ground for building community, traction, and funding all at once. Platforms like Kickstarter, Indiegogo, and equity crowdfunding sites like Wefunder give you an unparalleled opportunity to rally supporters around your cause.

Take, for example, **Cleo AI**, an AI-driven financial assistant that initially raised seed funding through traditional routes but could have just as easily thrived in a crowdfunding environment. Why? Because the product solves a tangible, relatable problem—personal finance management—and uses AI in an accessible, consumer-facing way.

Crowdfunding works best when you:

1. Tell a Compelling Story

No one logs into Kickstarter hoping to fund "AI-Powered SaaS Platform v3.0." They back stories. Think about how you **felt** watching the underdog rise in movies like **Rudy** or **The Pursuit of Happyness**. That's the emotional core of successful crowdfunding campaigns. Share your journey—why are you passionate about this idea? Why are YOU the one person on Earth uniquely qualified to build it?

2. Show Tangible Progress

Crowdfunding isn't charity. Backers expect proof that their money is enabling real progress. If you can demonstrate early traction—whether it's a functional prototype, a working demo, or a handful of paying customers—you're far more likely to instill confidence.

3. Leverage Blatant Transparency

Crowdfunding backers aren't institutional investors—cater to their mindset. Share your thought process, your roadmap, even your mistakes. Transparency builds trust, and trust inspires investment.

Case in point: **Pebble**, the smartwatch that shattered Kickstarter records, didn't position itself as "the best wearable tech platform of the future." Instead, it was "the smartwatch that works for YOU." Solo AI entrepreneurs can adopt the same approach—humanizing your AI-driven product makes it relatable and fundable.

Bootstrapping: Grow Like a Lone Oak

Every entrepreneur is familiar with the lure of outside money—the shiny veneer of a Series A round, the glamour of big-name backers. Yet some of the most successful solo-built ventures were funded the hard way: by bootstrapping.

Bootstrapping—funding your business through existing revenue, personal savings, or strategic partnerships—requires a mindset best epitomized by the ethos of Harper Lee's **To Kill a Mockingbird**. Atticus Finch taught us that quiet perseverance can overcome incredible odds. As a bootstrapper, you embody this ethos by relying on creativity, resilience, and resourcefulness to outmaneuver better-funded competition.

Let's break down how to bootstrap an AI business as a solo entrepreneur:

1. Start Small, Aim Big

Don't get bogged down building the entire cathedral on Day 1. What's the simplest version of your product that demonstrates how your AI creates value? This is your MVP (minimum viable product). For instance, OpenAI didn't release GPT-4 from the get-go—it began modestly by publishing research and iterating incrementally.

2. Turn Clients into Financiers

If you're building an AI product for a specific niche—say, an AI tool for automating legal contracts—consider pre-selling it to potential clients. Offer them discounts for early adoption. This approach not only funds development but also validates your product-market fit.

3. Leverage No-Code or Low-Code Tools

Building an AI product doesn't mean you need to code an entire system from scratch. Platforms like Hugging Face, OpenAI APIs, and cloud services from AWS or Google Cloud offer ready-to-use frameworks for deploying machine learning models. The less time and money you spend reinventing the wheel, the faster you can monetize.

Challenging Questions: Where Do You Stand?

As you contemplate your next move in the fundraising journey, pause to ask yourself:

- What's My Funding Philosophy?

Am I comfortable bringing in outside investors, knowing they will have expectations—growth targets, possibly even board control? Or do I value control and independence above all else?

- Is My "AI Factor" Understood?

If I pitched my idea to my 90-year-old grandmother, could she understand the value and purpose of my AI application? If not, how can I simplify my narrative and sharpen my pitch?

- Am I Creating Value for a Cause Larger than Myself?

Fundraising isn't just about money—it's about resonance. Do I believe in my product enough to rally investors, backers, or customers to my vision?

The Unicorn Blueprint Starts Here

Fundraising as a solo AI entrepreneur isn't about proving doubters wrong—it's about proving believers right. Whether you choose the VC route, take the bootstrap path, or stand on the shoulders of crowdfunding platforms, your ability to convey clarity, conviction, and passion is your greatest asset.

At the end of **The Great Gatsby**, Nick writes, "Gatsby believed in the green light, the orgastic future that year by year recedes before us." As a solo AI founder, your green light is closer than you think. Investors, customers, and supporters are waiting not just to believe in your vision—but to invest in it. Will you give them a reason to?

It's time to stop standing in the field and start planting seeds that will grow into something extraordinary. This is your funding moment. Make it count.

CHAPTER 16

HOW TO LEVERAGE GLOBAL AI TALENT AT LOW COSTS

Imagine you're standing on the porch of Jay Gatsby's mansion, looking out at the green light across the bay. That light— gleaming and distant—represents your dream of building a unicorn business as a solo founder. It burns bright, but between you and it lies a churning sea of complexity, resource constraints, and the ever-looming specter of burnout. You're one person, staring down the colossal task of turning an idea into a thriving enterprise. The question is: how do you cross the bay? How do you harness the infinite potential the world offers and get closer to your dream, without capsizing your boat in the process?

The answer may surprise you: it's not about working harder; it's about working smarter. And in today's world, there are two game-changing ways to do that—**artificial intelligence** and **global talent**. The key lies in knowing how to marry these two forces in a way that brings you maximum efficiency and creativity without breaking the bank. This chapter is your blueprint for doing exactly that.

Redefining Solo: The Amplified Founder

Gone are the days when being a solo founder meant working in isolation. As Toni Morrison wrote, "If you want to fly, you have to give up the things that weigh you down." Solo doesn't have to mean solitary. Today, you have a global workforce at your fingertips—an infinite well of talent accessible through platforms like Upwork, Toptal, Fiverr, and GitHub. Layer on top of that an evolving ecosystem of AI tools—from OpenAI's GPT to no-code tools like Zapier—and suddenly, you're not "going it alone."

You're building a team. A team that works remotely, scales dynamically, and can fit neatly within the smallest of budgets.

But here's the rub: there's a skill to this. It's not just about scouting talent or downloading an AI tool. It's about creating a powerful symphony where people and algorithms play in harmony. Today, I'll guide you through how to become the conductor of this orchestra.

Case Study: The Curious Tale of Jake, the Solo SaaS Founder

Let's start with a real-life story. Jake was a UX designer based in Austin. He had an idea for a SaaS (Software as a Service) tool that could streamline project management for small creative agencies. He didn't know how to code, didn't have deep pockets, and he certainly didn't know how to build a tech stack. But instead of tucking his dream away, Jake got resourceful.

Step one: he saved $1,000 as seed money. Then he logged onto Upwork and posted a job for an AI engineer in India to build a prototype of the product's core algorithm. Within 24 hours, he had ten bids ranging from $500 to $1,800, and after interviewing the candidates, he chose one with a portfolio stocked with AI projects. They worked together through Zoom and Slack, refining the prototype until it was functional.

Step two: Jake subscribed to Zapier for $50/month to automate several key functions and reduce the amount of manual labor needed for his operations. He was now doing the work of an entire team, but with just himself, one remote programmer, and a handful of affordable tools. The best part? When the prototype failed to resonate with his initial beta users, pivoting was inexpensive. He iterated quickly, revising the algorithm based on user feedback, and within six months, his SaaS tool was live. Today, Jake's platform makes $80,000 in monthly recurring revenue, and he's still a solo founder.

What can we learn from Jake? Two things:

1. You don't need to hire full-time employees to build something transformative.
2. Leveraging global freelancers and AI tools creates a level playing field for underfunded founders.

Now let's break down exactly how you can replicate Jake's success.

Step 1: Narrow Your Focus

Before you jump onto freelancing platforms or start experimenting with AI, you need clarity. What's the one thing your business needs right now that you can't do alone? Be ruthless in defining this. Remember what Hemingway said: "But man is not made for defeat. A man can be destroyed but not defeated." The same is true for founders. Spread yourself too thin, and you'll destroy your focus. But by zeroing in on one thing, you can overcome even the steepest obstacle.

Are you stuck because you don't know how to code? Hire a developer. Do you need a marketing strategy? Find a growth hacker. Do you want to automate customer service functions? Explore AI chatbots like Intercom or ChatGPT-powered APIs.

Clarity is your north star because it helps you identify the exact kind of talent or tool you need and ensures that every dollar you spend has highest impact.

Step 2: How to Find and Vet Global Freelancers

Global talent isn't just cheap; it's diverse, dynamic, and brimming with unexpected insights. But finding the right fit requires some finesse. Here's how to do it effectively:

1. Use the Right Platforms:

- Upwork and Fiverr are great for individual freelancers.
- Toptal focuses on top-tier talent, though it comes at a higher price point.
- GitHub is an excellent place to scout developers by studying their project contributions.

2. Evaluate More Than Just Cost:

Many founders make the mistake of going for the cheapest option. Don't. Look at candidates holistically: their portfolio, reviews, and ability to communicate effectively. The best freelancers are those who demonstrate ownership over a project—they think beyond tasks and care about outcomes.

3. Start Small:

Begin with a trial project. This minimizes your risk and gives you a sense of the freelancer's dedication, creativity, and technical skills without committing to a long-term arrangement.

Example: A Modest Start

A friend of mine, Sarah, wanted to create an AI-powered budgeting app. She hired a graphic designer from Serbia for $200 to design mockups for her app's interface and an AI engineer from Bangladesh for $600 to build a basic machine-learning model. Every step of her project was modular—starting with small hires allowed her to build momentum over time, testing each component of her vision without blowing her savings.

Step 3: Supercharging Your Team with AI Tools

AI tools aren't just shiny toys for techies—they're the workhorses in your solo-founder toolbox. Think of these tools as the fictional Yoda to your Luke Skywalker: they don't replace the hero, they enable the hero to unlock their full potential.

Here are several AI tools to consider integrating into your workflow:

- **Customer Support:** Use ChatGPT or Intercom's AI chatbots to provide 24/7 customer service for a fraction of the cost of a human team.
- **Marketing Automation**: Tools like Jasper.ai or Copy.ai can help you write ad copy, blog posts, and email campaigns in minutes.

- **Data Analysis:** Tools like MonkeyLearn or RapidMiner enable you to turn raw customer feedback into actionable insights.
- **No-Code Builders:** Platforms like Bubble let you create apps without ever writing a line of code.

The genius of these tools is that they automate the repetitive, mundane tasks that would otherwise drain your energy. More importantly, they free you up to focus on creative and strategic thinking.

Step 4: The Art of Collaboration

By now, you might have assembled a small army of freelancers and AI tools, but here's the paradox: you still need to lead. Simply delegating tasks won't cut it. Think of yourself as the captain steering a ship while still trimming the sails.

How do you ensure your distributed team stays aligned?

1. Over-Communicate Your Vision:

People—whether freelancers or permanent hires—work better when they feel connected to the larger purpose. Regularly remind your team why you're doing what you're doing. As Simon Sinek would say, "Start with why."

2. Set Clear Deliverables:

Freelancers thrive on clarity. Provide explicit instructions, deadlines, and success metrics so there's no guesswork about what you're looking for.

3. Hold Weekly Stand-Ups:

Even in the most asynchronous setups, a weekly Zoom or Slack check-in is invaluable. Use it to align priorities, review progress, and recalibrate.

Asking the Big Questions

Before we end this chapter, let's turn the spotlight back to you:

- Are you truly willing to let go of the need for control, trusting a global team and AI tools to execute your vision?
- Are you willing to experiment, fail, and iterate—just like Jake and Sarah?
- And perhaps most importantly, are you willing to do the inner work required to lead with clarity and purpose, even when resources are tight?

Jay Gatsby saw his green light as a symbol of hope. But the light only came closer to those who dared to sail toward it—not alone, but with a well-curated crew. As a solo founder, your job is not to row every oar yourself. It's to leverage AI and the global workforce with intelligence, creativity, and heart.

The question now is not whether you will achieve your dream, but how smartly you're willing to chart the course.

Your green light awaits. Sail wisely.

CHAPTER 17

CRACKING THE
AI MARKETING REVOLUTION

I n Frank Herbert's **Dune**, one of the most resonant lines is, "Fear is the mind-killer." For entrepreneurs and marketers venturing into the AI revolution, fear—or in most cases, resistance—is what stands in the way of leveraging its full power. Today, AI isn't just an accessory to your marketing strategy; it's the engine. The days of intuition-based marketing are dwindling fast. In their place stands a world where data-driven decisions, amplified by the precision of artificial intelligence, promise to unlock the kind of growth that once seemed mythical.

But let's pause and ask the uncomfortable question: Are you afraid of embracing AI because it feels foreign, technical, or even out of your ethical comfort zone? The truth is, those emotional barriers are the only thing standing between your business and exponential growth. By the end of this chapter, you'll not only understand how AI is transforming marketing but also feel empowered to wield it with intent and mastery.

Let's break down this revolution into three parts: how AI helps you know your customer better than they know themselves, how it optimizes and personalizes campaigns, and, finally, how it can predict behavior in ways that border on clairvoyance.

AI Marketing as a Mirror to the Soul of Your Customer

In **The Great Gatsby**, F. Scott Fitzgerald paints a stark yet mesmerizing image of Jay Gatsby, a man who meticulously tailored every aspect of his life to win Daisy's love. Imagine being able to match your customer with the same tenacity—but without the tragic flaws and guesswork Gatsby succumbed to. AI, in essence, offers that power. It is your ultimate mirror to understand the desires, motivations, and pain points of your customers.

Consider Netflix. At its core, Netflix isn't a streaming service; it's a data-driven juggernaut. Every time you binge-watch a series or abandon a movie halfway through, the platform learns something about you. Netflix leverages AI to predict what you're likely to want next, serving personalized recommendations that feel eerily on-point. This predictive intelligence has created not just a product, but an experience—and it's a key reason why over 230 million people can't quit their subscriptions. Netflix is no Gatsby; its love for its consumers is powered by data-fueled action, ensuring continuous connection and engagement.

Now, ask yourself: Do you truly understand your customers in the way Netflix understands its users? Or are you still working off personas that feel vague, outdated, or hypothetical? AI allows you to move beyond generalized demographics into psychographics and predictive insights. For example, instead of targeting "males, ages 18-25, living in urban areas," AI will reveal, "This group of males has a high preference for short-form Instagram content featuring playful humor and under $50 price points." The journey from a generic blueprint to a vivid masterpiece is entirely orchestrated by AI.

Tools like IBM Watson Marketing and Salesforce Einstein are already helping brands paint the clearest possible picture of their audience. Watson can analyze sentiment in real-time social media conversations, showing brands exactly what people think and feel about their products. This is empathy at scale—a superpower you can channel. Even with accessible tools like ChatGPT, just prompt it to act like your buyer persona or your ideal customer profile (ICP) and get all the answers to questions you never dared to ask.

Here's an exercise: Don't think about your "target market." Think about your **target individual**. What do they eat for breakfast? Why do they feel anxious at 8 PM? Which podcasts do they follow? AI can answer these questions—not in a hypothetical or abstract way, but grounded in real, actionable data. It's not clairvoyance; it's just advanced pattern recognition.

Optimization On Steroids: The Automaton Within

Imagine an inexperienced baker attempting to whip up a layered cake without any set recipe. That's what many marketers were doing pre-AI. They tried campaign after campaign, burning calories, money, and time, but the layers rarely aligned. AI adds not just a recipe but the hands of a Michelin-starred chef to the process.

Take the example of Heineken. The company wanted to experiment with using AI to enhance its "Cities" campaign, which involved hyper-targeted ads designed to inspire audiences to explore their cities via Heineken-sponsored events. Using AI from Google Cloud, the company didn't just optimize these concepts— they redefined the entire process. AI was able to split-test thousands of potential ad variations, tweaking headlines, imagery, and offers in milliseconds based on real-time engagement metrics. This left Heineken with ads that weren't just "better" but genuinely resonant with individual audience segments.

Another monumental leap came from The North Face. By integrating IBM Watson, North Face created an AI tool to recommend products based on conversational inputs. A shopper could log onto their site and say, "I need a jacket for hiking in Alaska this December." Watson, processing the weather and user preferences, would instantly recommend a suitable product. That's not just personalization; that's a concierge-level experience most consumers didn't think was possible. And also here you could use consumer level tools like WhatsApp business cloud or Meta's messenger as a platform to deliver an assistant GPT chatbot from OpenAI trained on your data.

These stories are not outliers. This level of optimization and personalization is accessible to you when you start exploring AI-driven ad platforms like Adzooma or Albert AI. These platforms absorb your marketing data—click-through rates, consumer demographics, historical performance—and churn out smarter, leaner campaigns in real time. They're not designed to replace your creativity; they're designed to amplify it.

Now, a word to the wise: Automation isn't mindless execution. It's delegation. Don't fall for the trap of "set it and forget it." Instead, treat AI like a collaborator—a digital partner that executes at the speed of light but still requires the strategic oversight that only a human visionary like you can provide.

Predictive Insights: The Crystal Ball

Let me take you to 2002. Steven Spielberg's **Minority Report** delighted and unnerved audiences with a vision of personalized advertising. Tom Cruise's character walks through a mall as holographic ads shout his name and display products tailored to his past purchases. At the time, it seemed creepy and far-fetched. Today, it's a reality hiding in plain sight.

An obvious example? Amazon. Its AI doesn't just recommend products you might want—it predicts your future buying behavior. "Customers who bought this also bought..." is more than harmless upselling. Behind the scenes, Amazon's algorithms cross-reference millions of data points to understand patterns you may not even be aware of. For instance, if you've just bought a baby stroller, Amazon knows there's a good chance you'll need diapers in the near future. In some cases, it will offer these products before you can even type them into the search bar. This is predictive AI in action.

Smaller companies are getting in on this game too. My favorite case study is Stitch Fix, a clothing subscription service. Their AI algorithm combines consumer preferences, style quizzes, and purchase data to handpick new wardrobe items. This "crystal ball" allowed the company to leapfrog traditional retail and build a billion-dollar subscription-based business. Importantly, Stitch Fix combines AI with human stylists to enhance accuracy. It's the perfect marriage of human creativity and machine learning.

Let's turn the mirror on you again. Are you using analytics reactively—tracking what customers have already done—or proactively—predicting their next move? With tools like Google

Analytics 4 or Shopify's AI-driven segmentation tools, even solo entrepreneurs can start leaping into forward-looking insights. AI doesn't just show you the present; it's a flashlight illuminating the road ahead.

Here's a quick exercise: List five ways you could anticipate your customers' needs. Could you preemptively offer complementary products? Could you leverage sentiment analysis to detect when dissatisfaction is brewing? These small but powerful applications of predictive AI could be the difference between fading into irrelevance and becoming indispensable to your market.

The Ethical Giant in the Room

Now, it would be remiss not to address the ethical elephant—or perhaps the ethical giant—in the room. AI's unparalleled access to data comes with responsibility. Consumers are becoming more aware of how their information is being gathered and used. Your task is to build trust, not violate it.

Apple has expertly woven transparency into their brand by emphasizing privacy over profit. Their ad, "What Happens on Your iPhone, Stays on Your iPhone" struck a chord in a world increasingly filled with data breaches and Big Brother fears. This is no accident. Apple's commitment to responsible data use serves as a reminder: In adopting AI, you cannot forsake ethics.

Trust is fragile, and the line between "helpful predictions" and "invasive stalking" can blur quickly. Use AI as a tool, not a weapon. Be transparent about its role in your marketing strategy. Customers appreciate personalization but resent manipulation. The good news? By focusing on genuine value creation, you'll sidestep most ethical pitfalls.

The Call to Action

I'll end this chapter with a challenge: Step into the shoes of your 21st-century customer. Demanding, impatient, and overwhelmed, they won't settle for mediocrity. Will you insist on wooing them with guesses and gut instincts? Or will you rise to the occasion by using AI to listen deeply, act swiftly, and think ahead?

AI in marketing is not a passing trend. It's the new normal—the language of modern connection. Let's make one thing crystal clear: You don't need to be a tech wizard to harness this power. You just need the courage to experiment, the discipline to learn, and the humility to let data guide you.

Because in this revolution, one quintessential truth remains: The businesses that thrive will be the ones that know their customers better, faster, and deeper than anyone else. And now, thanks to AI, that business could—and should—be yours.

CHAPTER 18

CYBERSECURITY
FOR SOLO UNICORNS

Somewhere in the hallowed pages of American literature, in F. Scott Fitzgerald's **The Great Gatsby**, there's a poignant observation: "They were careless people, Tom and Daisy— they smashed up things and creatures and then retreated back into their money or their vast carelessness, or whatever it was that kept them together, and let other people clean up the mess they had made." For solo entrepreneurs who aim to build a unicorn enterprise, this line serves as both cautionary tale and call to action. In a world driven by data and AI, carelessness in managing operational security can cause irreparable damage—not just to your own venture, but to those who depend on it. Unlike Tom and Daisy, solo unicorns can't afford to retreat into carelessness or rely on others to fix their mess.

In this chapter, we're going to explore one of the pillars of solo entrepreneurship in the age of AI: cybersecurity. Your customer data, intellectual property, and even the operational viability of your business depend on how well you shield your enterprise from cyber threats. This isn't just about owning antivirus software; it's about building a fortress from the ground up—a fortress that protects what you've worked so hard to create.

Why Cybersecurity Matters More Than Ever for Solo Unicorns

Imagine you're Frodo Baggins in **The Lord of the Rings**. Your enterprise is the One Ring—not inherently dangerous, but highly coveted by malevolent forces. Without robust protection, your business becomes a target. Small businesses and solo enterprises often assume they won't attract the attention of hackers because they're "too small to matter." This is a dangerous myth.

According to a study by Verizon, 43% of cyberattacks target small businesses, many of which are deemed attractive because they lack the resources of larger corporations. As a solo unicorn, you are potentially sitting on proprietary processes, valuable customer data, or innovative algorithms that bigger players—or bad actors—would find advantageous to exploit.

Consider the example of a freelance AI consultant we'll call "Jennifer." She designed a proprietary machine-learning model that improved supply chains for small retailers by 25%. Her work attracted attention, but not all of it was good. One day, she logged into her project management suite to find that her system had been compromised. All her data—months of hard work—was encrypted. A hacker demanded $40,000 in Bitcoin. Worse still, they had accessed sensitive client information, placing her reputation in jeopardy. Jennifer didn't have a recovery plan, and it cost her the trust of key clients, who moved their business elsewhere.

There is no room for complacency. A breach isn't just about a financial hit or downtime; it's about trust, reputation, and your ability to continue operating at all.

The Three Core Areas of Cybersecurity for Solo Entrepreneurs

To prepare yourself for a secure journey, you need to focus on three core areas: prevention, resilience, and mitigation. Think of cybersecurity as your business's "immune system." Prevention is like washing your hands and avoiding crowded flu-season gatherings. Resilience involves stocking up on vitamins to boost your immune system. And mitigation? That's making sure you've got antibiotics on hand if you do catch an infection. Let's explore these in detail.

1. Prevention: Fortifying the Gates

The first and most important aspect of cybersecurity is prevention. How do you ensure that malicious actors can't even make it through the gates of your digital fortress?

Passwords Are Your First Line of Defense—but They Aren't Enough

You wouldn't leave your front door unlocked, but many solo entrepreneurs do something just as dangerous in the digital realm. Weak passwords are one of the most common ways hackers gain access to systems.

You might think you're safe with "correcthorsebatterystaple" or the name of your favorite sports team. You're not. Password managers like 1Password, Dashlane, or LastPass make it easy to generate and store complex strings, without trusting your memory. But don't stop there. Enable multi-factor authentication (MFA) wherever possible. MFA is like adding a second deadbolt to your front door—an extra step that makes an intruder's life far harder.

Update Relentlessly

One of the most famous cybersecurity breaches in recent history was the Equifax breach in 2017, which exposed the personal data of over 143 million people. How did it happen? Equifax failed to update a vulnerability in one of their open-source software libraries—a lapse that cost them millions in fines and an irreparably damaged reputation.

For a solo unicorn, the lesson is clear: updates are not optional. Be obsessive about updating your software. Whether it's your operating system, website plugins, or even your router firmware, assume every outdated system is a potential backdoor for hackers.

Invest in AI-Powered Security Tools

AI isn't just a tool for automating your business; it's also a weapon for protecting it. Tools like Cylance and Darktrace use AI to monitor your network for unusual activity. Think of it as having a smart guard dog—not just barking at every shadow but sniffing out credible threats before they materialize.

2. Resilience: Building An Anti-Fragile Business

If prevention is your shield, resilience is your ability to take punches and keep standing. In today's cybersecurity landscape, it's not a question of **if** you'll be targeted, but **when**.

Backups Are Your Lifeline

Imagine you're writing the next great American novel, only for your hard drive to crash halfway through. Would you risk losing years of work to chance? As a solo unicorn, backups are your manuscript's salvation.

Adopt the "3-2-1" rule:

- Keep **3** copies of your data.
- Store them in **2** different formats (e.g., cloud and external hard drives).
- Ensure at least **1** is stored offsite.

Services like Backblaze or Acronis can automate this for you. And don't forget to test your backups regularly. It's useless to have backups you can't restore.

Case Study: The Resilience of a Solo Content Creator

Meet Daniel, a solo YouTuber specializing in financial literacy content. In 2022, his channel was hacked. The attackers deleted all his videos—years of hard work seemed gone in an instant. Fortunately, Daniel had adhered to the 3-2-1 backup rule. Within 48 hours, his channel was restored, and he even managed to release a new video addressing the breach, which garnered record views. His audience appreciated the transparency and watched his business bounce back stronger.

What would Daniel's career have looked like if he hadn't prioritized resilience?

3. Mitigation: Preparing for the Unthinkable

Even with robust prevention and resilience strategies, breaches can still happen. As the philosopher Mike Tyson famously said, "Everyone has a plan until they get punched in the face." How you mitigate damage determines whether your solo unicorn survives a crisis—or crumbles under pressure.

Incident Response Plan (IRP): Your Cybersecurity Playbook

When the unimaginable happens, an Incident Response Plan is your guide to taking control instead of panicking. This plan should include:

- A clear chain of communication. Who do you contact first? (Hint: Law enforcement and your web hosting provider.)
- Steps to contain the breach. Stop further damage by disconnecting affected systems.
- Customer communication templates. Transparency builds trust. Inform customers quickly about what happened and what actions you've taken.

Cyber-Liability Insurance: An Often Overlooked Lifesaver

We insure our homes, cars, and health—but what about our businesses? Cyber-liability insurance can cover expenses like legal fees, notification costs, and even ransomware payments. Speak with a specialist who understands the needs of small digital businesses.

Concluding Thoughts: The Cost of Carelessness

Walt Whitman, that great chronicler of life's infinite possibilities, once wrote, "Keep your face always toward the sunshine—and shadows will fall behind you." As a solo unicorn, you may be tempted to focus solely on growth, innovation, or customer acquisition—the sunshine of your business. But neglecting cybersecurity is inviting the shadow to catch up with you.

To close this chapter, I'll ask you this: How much is your business worth to you? Not just in terms of finances, but in terms of your dreams, your freedom, and your impact on the world. Now, measure that against the relatively modest cost of fortifying your operational security.

Building a unicorn enterprise isn't just about reaching extraordinary heights; it's about protecting the foundation you stand on. Your business deserves a stronghold—so start building it today.

CHAPTER 19

DESIGNING INTUITIVE AI PRODUCTS FOR USERS

I n Ernest Hemingway's **The Old Man and the Sea**, Santiago—the aging fisherman—clashes with both the ocean and himself. His interaction with the vast, mysterious sea is not unlike how most users experience AI for the first time: full of promise, potential, but shrouded in ambiguity. Santiago's journey reminds us that to navigate the vast unknown, we need the right tools and simplicity in design. AI, like the ocean, only becomes manageable when we build the right boat to cross it.

The critical challenge for entrepreneurs, designers, and engineers alike is to create AI products that feel as intuitive as an oar to a sailor's hand. Done right, these tools amplify human potential rather than overwhelm or alienate us. Seamlessness is not just a feature—it is the foundation of trust in an age where complexity can so easily create barriers.

The mechanics of designing for artificial intelligence bring us into an intersection of human-centered design and cutting-edge technology. This chapter is dedicated to helping you architect AI products that enrich lives meaningfully—where form, function, and intelligence blend so elegantly that the experience feels inevitable, as natural as breathing.

Simplicity is Not Simplicity; It's Empathy

Let's start with what "simplicity" really means. While many interpret simplicity as stripping down features to their bare minimum, in reality, simplicity in AI design is about reducing **cognitive friction**. It's the ability to understand what a user truly needs—and eliminate unnecessary distractions. This isn't minimalism as an aesthetic; it's minimalism of effort for the user.

Take Netflix's recommendation engine again. The brilliance of its system is not just its algorithm but its frictionlessness for users. The homepage doesn't overwhelm you with rows upon rows of genres or piles of instructions about how AI selects movies for you. Instead, it simply shows you something you're likely to enjoy, suggesting, "You might like this." Users only experience the outcome of a sophisticated AI engine, not the machinery behind the scenes.

But here's a question for you: Are your AI products reducing cognitive load, or are you making users work harder to understand what your technology is providing? Imagine you walked into a library, and instead of being able to browse books organized under clear genres, you were handed a pile of unsorted titles. Would you feel empowered or frustrated?

To design well, you must ask yourself constantly: How do you give clarity where others create chaos and anticipation where others breed anxiety?

Here's a metaphor for you to hold onto: Great AI design should feel like GPS navigation. It anticipates your next move, recalculates when unexpected obstacles arise, and speaks to you in terms of meaningful actions, not technical jargon. "Turn left in 500 feet" is helpful; "Your coordinates deviate by 2.5 degrees" is not. Is your product equivalent to that GPS voice?

The Hidden Genius of Default States: The Principle of Invisible Intelligence

In the novel **To Kill a Mockingbird**, Atticus Finch says, "You never really understand a person until you consider things from his point of view... until you climb into his skin and walk around in it." The same holds true for successful AI product design. If users have to constantly press buttons, type commands, or manually train models, they'll be more likely to abandon your product.

Digital products must try to interpret users' needs before users even articulate them—a process we often refer to as creating intelligent "default states." AI is most magical and sticky when it works invisibly in the background, anticipating problems or choices before they arise.

Take Google Photos, for instance. Its AI auto-tags memories, categorizes faces, and even offers to create albums when it detects you've been at a wedding or vacation. This "invisible intelligence" respects users' unspoken desires. The product saves time, strengthens emotional connections to memories, and does so without demanding input.

Tesla's Autopilot provides another example. By default, the system eases into decisions based on user behavior. For instance, it anticipates speed bumps and adjusts accordingly. A Tesla driver doesn't need to toggle dozens of parameters; the car knows when to slow down.

Think about your own AI product blueprint. Does your AI relieve workload by doing the heavy lifting? Or does it require users to juggle levers, buttons, and knobs to wrangle it into utility?

Ask yourself: Is your AI operating like an eloquent assistant, intuitively adaptive to the user's intent? Or is it like an unruly intern, requiring constant babysitting?

Designing for Human Connection: The Emotional Layer of AI

At its heart, every great product connects not just to our minds but also to our hearts. AI might be a complex mathematical construct, but its purpose is fundamentally emotional—it enables joy, wonder, or relief. Designing this emotional layer means building trust and empathy into every pixel, interaction, and decision tree.

Duolingo, for instance, turns what could feel like a sterile experience into something deeply engaging. Learners interact with a persistent, cheerful AI mascot that motivates them to return every day. It's not just teaching Spanish—it's creating a relationship. The app's tone, gamified achievements, and delightful nudges are all meticulously designed for emotional resonance, not just functionality.

Now, contrast this with an airline's virtual assistant chatbot that coldly spits out FAQ responses under the guise of "helping." While powered by AI, such tools fall flat because they lack empathy—they are functional, yes, but largely indifferent to the user's frustrations.

A word of caution: Never let the algorithms inside the machine drown out the humanity on the outside. Remember, your users aren't connecting with the ones and zeros—they're connecting with you.

Consider how conversational AI—like Amazon Alexa or Apple's Siri—feels approachable because their creators intentionally designed them to feel personable. From their polite responses to the subtle humor layered into their interactions, these products demonstrate that relatability is just as valuable a design goal as accuracy.

Challenge: Write down the words you want users to use when they describe interacting with your AI product. Is it "comforting"? "Exciting"? "Magical"? Then ask yourself: Does your design actively evoke those feelings?

Avoid Decision Paralysis: Less Choice, More Guidance

The classic American author William Faulkner once said, "You cannot swim for new horizons until you have courage to lose sight of the shore." Translating this to design: Users shouldn't have to cling to the shore of micromanagement when interacting with your AI product. Yet all too often, we overwhelm them with too many options.

Spotify is a perfect case study in limiting choice thoughtfully. Rather than forcing users to sort through vast song libraries every time they want to listen, Spotify's AI curates playlists like "Discover Weekly" and "Release Radar," crafted specifically for their tastes. The fewer decisions a user has to make, the more pleasurable and frictionless the experience becomes.

Amazon's recommendation engine similarly doesn't just suggest products—it guides purchasing decisions by offering streamlined options that make sense based on users' browsing and buying history.

On the flip side, open-ended AI tools—like ChatGPT—can occasionally suffer from decision fatigue. They ask users to input "any question" or "give any task," which can feel paralyzing to newcomers. Successful iterations of these tools include use-case templates (e.g., "write a marketing headline" or "help me brainstorm") to ease first-time interactions.

Pro Tip: When in doubt, offer guidance over choice. What pre-designed pathways can you include to help your users feel confident in getting started?

Measure the Magic: Iteration and Feedback Loops

Design simplicity doesn't stop once the product ships. Much like Hemingway revising his novels, you need iteration to reach excellence. When Hemingway revised **The Old Man and the Sea**, he didn't add layers; instead, he stripped away redundancies until readers felt they were left with the purest, most essential narrative.

AI product design requires the same discipline. Successful businesses cultivate user feedback loops to continuously improve functionality, reduce unnecessary complexity, and optimize experiences. Consider YouTube's recommendation algorithm, which iteratively learns not just from billions of users' behavior but also from designers evaluating engagement metrics—a symbiosis of human intention and automated learning.

But how will **you** measure success? Is your AI product solving a problem users care deeply about? Does it get smarter and more intuitive over time, or is your AI stagnant—repeating the same patterns without genuine evolution?

Building an Intuitive AI Ecosystem: Pulling It All Together

Here's the cornerstone truth: An intuitive AI product is born at the intersection of **understanding human needs**, **removing pain points**, and **delivering results effortlessly**. It is not just about creating robust algorithms. It's about designing technology that disappears and delivers value.

Take Apple's Face ID as the final example. It is the epitome of intuitive AI design. Users don't care about facial landmark detection or the neural engines behind it. They care about unlocking their phones without thinking, without hesitation, and without error. The technology works so seamlessly that it fades into the background of the user's experience—becoming **invisible**.

Endlessly tinkering with technical features alone won't get you there. To quote Faulkner once more: "Always dream and shoot higher than you know you can do."

What's your horizon? What's your bold vision? Is the AI you're building not only solving functional problems but leaving emotional resonance in its wake?

Remember: Human lives are complex enough. The ocean is vast. Your product must be the boat—and the clearer, simpler, and more intuitive that design, the greater chance you have of helping someone sail forward into possibility.

CHAPTER 20

THE AI MONETIZATION FLYWHEEL

When I first stumbled upon the concept of compounding, I was sitting in a stiff-backed chair in a dimly lit college lecture hall, half-listening to a somewhat monotone professor explain the magic of compound interest. He drew an upward curve on the board—exponential growth, he called it—a visual meant to inspire awe for the power of reinvestment over time. I'll admit it didn't inspire awe in me at the time. But years later, when I watched organizations grow from garage startups into billion-dollar unicorns powered by disciplined reinvestment, I realized just how powerful that lesson was. It wasn't just true for savings accounts or investment portfolios. It was true for businesses everywhere, particularly for the new breed of solo entrepreneurs building AI-driven unicorn companies.

In this chapter, we'll talk about a mechanism I call **The AI Monetization Flywheel**. It's a process for taking early momentum in your solo business—perhaps your first $10,000 or $100,000 in revenue—and reinvesting it strategically to create compounding growth. The flywheel thrives on reinvestment and deliberate scaling—a little momentum today can become unstoppable force tomorrow.

This is not just theoretical. Beyond being a cool analogy, the flywheel is a practical blueprint for scaling your AI-driven business into something exceptional. Think of it as turning a great story into a never-ending epic—the kind that drives both financial freedom and meaningful impact. And like any great protagonist in a piece of timeless American literature, it starts with choices you make at pivotal crossroads. Are you ready to take that first spin?

What is the Monetization Flywheel?

Author Jim Collins, in his classic book **Good to Great,** offers us the metaphor of the flywheel in corporate strategy. The premise is simple: build momentum slowly but surely, and over time, the energy you've generated creates self-reinforcing growth.

Let's make this concept even more tangible by examining it through the lens of AI monetization. At its core, the AI Monetization Flywheel works like this:

1. **Validate and launch your monetizable product or service.** (e.g., a GPT-powered copywriting tool, a personalized AI assistant, or a niche recommendation system.)
2. **Generate early revenue by solving a specific problem for a specific audience.** (Zero in on your high-value use cases and early adopters.)
3. **Reinvest that revenue strategically into growth levers** like product improvement, customer acquisition, or automation optimization.
4. **Use the reinvestment to improve your offering, delight your customers, and widen your market reach.**
5. **Scale iteratively** by repeating the process, compounding the gains with every spin.

Think about your flywheel like Hemingway's iceberg principle. What the reader—or, rather, your audience—sees on the surface is a sleek, cutting-edge product that seems effortless. But underneath lies the deeper foundation: relentless strategy, disciplined reinvestment, and a deeper understanding of the mechanics that keep the wheel turning.

Let's piece this process together step-by-step, testing it against real-world examples, and see how it fits into your journey as a solo unicorn founder.

Step 1: Start by Solving a Needlepoint Problem

Here's some good news: the flywheel doesn't suddenly appear from nowhere. It's ignited with small wins, which is where you come in.

Think of the AI Monetization Flywheel as a single snowball rolling down a hill. For solo entrepreneurs, it often starts with solving a narrow, impactful problem using AI. You don't need a broad, sweeping vision initially—in fact, narrowing your scope allows you to gain traction faster.

Consider **Jasper.ai**, one of the first prominent AI content creation tools powered by GPT-3. Jasper's founders didn't set out to replace all human writers; their initial focus was far more specific. They zoomed in on helping copywriters and marketers write marketing materials faster and with better quality. They chose a well-defined audience with a glaring problem, launched a simple product, and created immediate value. Early customers started writing better Facebook ads in half the time. The solution was simple but powerful, and it brought in paying customers almost from day one.

In your case, what problem are you solving? Is it helping ecommerce stores write better product descriptions? Or perhaps assisting financial planners in summarizing regulatory updates? Challenge yourself to answer the question: **What single, specific problem can only my AI-powered solution solve?** The narrower your field of focus early on, the faster you can find paying users who are desperate for your value.

Step 2: Leverage Early Revenue as Investment Capital

Too many entrepreneurs fall into the trap of spending all their early revenue on themselves. A nice office, a new gadget, a victory lap vacation—while rewarding yourself can feel good momentarily, it can kill momentum just as quickly.

The AI flywheel requires discipline. Every dollar that comes in during these early stages is sacred. That cash is the fuel that sends the flywheel spinning faster. As you think about reinvestment, ask one critical question:

What reinvestment will most quickly create a better customer experience or a wider audience for my product?

Imagine Netflix in its early days. When Reed Hastings was running a DVD-by-mail subscription service, he reinvested back into the customer experience—faster shipping, wider DVD selection, and easier browsing. He could have pocketed the profits, but instead, every reinvested dollar helped Netflix strengthen its position in a rapidly evolving market. Eventually, that discipline became the DNA that allowed Netflix to outcompete Blockbuster and scale its on-demand streaming empire.

For solo unicorn founders running AI businesses, reinvestment might mean hiring an external contractor to clean messy datasets, doubling down on marketing a breakthrough TikTok video ad campaign, or paying for advanced AI infrastructure to improve your system's response speed by 10X. Every dollar you strategically reinvest in growth today compounds into strength tomorrow.

Step 3: Automate to Accelerate

There's a reason this chapter is called **The AI Monetization Flywheel:** it leans on technology to win. At its essence, the solo unicorn enterprise depends on highly scalable systems—and no system scales more efficiently than automation and AI.

Consider Brian Chesky and Joe Gebbia in the formative years of Airbnb. Their growth flywheel didn't find momentum until they automated key parts of their process—most importantly, reliable matchmaking for users and hosts. Airbnb's customer acquisition and onboarding capabilities became a well-oiled machine, allowing them to reach millions without requiring massive manual input.

As a solo unicorn, you may already be using AI tools like Zapier, Make.com, OpenAI's APIs, Google Cloud, or AWS to automate complex tasks: lead generation, operational workflows, customer support, or even R&D. Take inventory of where you're bottlenecking your growth—customer service? Onboarding? Data labeling? Whatever it is, build automation into your reinvestment plan and free up time to focus on turning the flywheel faster.

Remember that reinvestment in automation isn't just a cost-saving move—it's also the creation of time leverage. Ask yourself:

What tasks would I be embarrassed to let a computer handle? Wherever that hesitation appears, dig deep. Automation might be your answer.

Step 4: The 10X Growth Move

At the heart of any flywheel is a multiplier effect. One reinvestment propels the next—until something clicks.

For Canva, the flywheel clicked when their early revenues enabled them to rapidly expand their suite of design tools, acquire user feedback, and turn Canva into an all-in-one platform adored by small businesses, educators, and individuals alike. They didn't stop at solving one problem; they expanded their reach progressively.

Your AI monetization flywheel will hit that breakout inflection point too—if you commit to amplifying what works. Let's say you've built an AI-powered virtual assistant skilled at customer service for local business owners. You begin with five beta testers but realize your top customer segment adores the time they save managing routine email replies. Reinvest early revenues into marketing campaigns targeting **just** that segment. Iterate based on their feedback. Build features specific to your ideal users, ride the wave of praise their success stories generate, expand to a bigger audience, and repeat.

Over time, the flywheel takes on a life of its own. Like something out of Steinbeck's **East of Eden**, customers and market dynamics begin doing the heavy lifting for you. Each referral feeds itself, and paid campaigns yield bigger ROIs. Each spin propels momentum forward faster.

Challenge for the reader: Will You Build It?

Somewhere right now, someone is staring at their fledgling AI-powered Slack bot, wondering if it's worth scaling. Or a translated language learning app with a handful of users. Maybe for you, it's a voice-controlled assistant with modest traction. The question is: will you let it grow?

The average person would take an early win as an excuse to coast. But I didn't write this blueprint for the average person. I wrote it for you—the solo entrepreneur ready to build something extraordinary.

So ask yourself:

- Are you narrowing your focus enough to validate the first spin of your flywheel?
- Are you safeguarding early revenues and reinvesting strategically for better customer outcomes?
- Are you systematically automating tasks that drain your time and energy?
- And more than anything, are you disciplined enough to weather the early grind and see compounding growth through?

Because here's the truth: every unicorn company started with just one spin of that flywheel.

In Gatsby's world, great enterprises might start with illusions of grandeur. In ours, they begin with deliberate choices, reinvestment, and the infinite loop of compounding momentum. Will you seize it?

Let's push that first spin together. See you at the top.

CHAPTER 21

REAL-WORLD CASE STUDIES: SOLO ENTREPRENEURS WHO MADE IT BIG

I n the vast and often turbulent ocean of entrepreneurship, there exists a rare breed of individuals who dare to set sail with no crew, no compass, and no lifeline but their own ingenuity. Solo entrepreneurs—those audacious enough to build businesses on their own—embody the very spirit of modern innovation. But what's truly remarkable is this: some of them don't just survive; they thrive. They turn their one-person operations into unicorn-level enterprises that radically disrupt industries and reset the parameters of what we think is possible. How do they do it? What lessons can we learn from their journeys?

This chapter profiles a handful of extraordinary solo entrepreneurs who built transformative companies from scratch, harnessing artificial intelligence (AI), creativity, and resilience. Their stories are more than just anecdotes—they're roadmaps. Like the heroes in great American literature, they faced their own dragons, battled self-doubt, and navigated the labyrinth of uncertainty, emerging not just victorious but profoundly changed. By peeling back the layers of their experiences, we uncover a common thread that every aspiring solo entrepreneur can weave into their tapestry of success.

Case Study 1: Pieter Levels – The Relentless Tinkerer Who Redefined Digital Nomadism

If there's any entrepreneur whose path reads like a character from Jack Kerouac's **On the Road**, it's Pieter Levels. A self-styled "digital nomad," Pieter began his entrepreneurial journey in 2013 with nothing but a laptop, a minimal budget, and an insatiable curiosity for building useful online tools. He didn't have a co-founder or a team—just a desire to create for the evolving world he inhabited.

Levels famously challenged himself to launch 12 startups in 12 months, an experiment in rapid execution. It wasn't about achieving perfection; it was about showing up every day, testing ideas, and letting the ones that resonated grow organically. His breakthrough came with **Nomad List**, a platform that ranks cities around the globe for remote workers. Suddenly, digital nomads worldwide had a resource that felt tailor-made for them, and Pieter had created a thriving online community.

Crucially, Pieter mastered the art of leveraging automation and AI to scale his one-person business. When people imagined nomadlife.com had a sprawling customer service team, they were unknowingly interacting with AI chatbot solutions. His mantra? Automate or die. Automation became his secret weapon, allowing him to focus on developing more ideas and products while still delivering an excellent user experience.

The Biggest Lesson: Start Before You're Ready

Pieter's story challenges us to bare our souls to imperfection. How often do we let fear stop us from sharing our work with the world? What dream has been sitting on your hard drive for months—or years—because you're too concerned it's not polished enough? Pieter reminds us that there's no applause for the ideas in our heads; execution is everything, and in the world of solo entrepreneurship, speed can be your greatest ally.

Case Study 2: Vanessa Lau – From Burnout to Building an Empowerment Empire

Vanessa Lau's story echoes themes you might find in a story by Toni Morrison, where personal pain is transformed into a beacon of empowerment for others. Vanessa didn't set out to become one of the most prominent names in content creation coaching; the path found her.

After leaving a corporate job that left her creatively and emotionally depleted, Vanessa doubled down on her passion for storytelling. Armed with little more than a camera and unwavering grit, she started posting free educational content on Instagram and YouTube. Within months, her authentic, no-frills advice on growing a personal brand started catching fire, and soon, Vanessa was earning six figures from her online coaching program.

Here's the twist: Vanessa ran everything herself. She understood that her value proposition wasn't technical gimmicks or elaborate production—it was **her**. Her personal relatability, coupled with smart use of accessible tech like Canva, online learning platforms like Kajabi, and AI-powered scheduling tools, helped her efficiently scale her operation. This allowed her to focus on consistently connecting with her audience without the chaos of managing a team.

Vanessa's story illustrates the power of alignment. The pain she felt in her previous life became the very fuel she used to create something meaningful and enduring. She's a living testament to the idea that when you build from a place of authenticity, success becomes inevitable.

The Biggest Lesson: Let Pain Drive Your Purpose

What if your greatest hardship is your greatest gift? What story are you uniquely qualified to tell, and how can you turn it into a robust business? Vanessa teaches us that our vulnerabilities are our superpowers—and when you blend them with action, they can lead to extraordinary results.

Case Study 3: Sahil Lavingia – The Artist Who Made Creativity a Business

Sahil Lavingia started out as a designer and software engineer. As an early employee of Pinterest, he found himself at the heartbeat of Silicon Valley's startup culture. But Sahil had his own vision: a world where creators could monetize their art directly, without middlemen taking a cut. So in 2011, Sahil launched **Gumroad**, a simple-but-powerful platform that allowed anyone to sell their work online. His dream was vivid, poetic even—he wanted to liberate creators from traditional gatekeepers.

Yet Sahil's journey was far from smooth. After raising venture capital and hiring a team, Gumroad hit a plateau. In 2015, he made the humbling decision to downsize: he laid off his staff, returned investor funds, and recalibrated the business as a one-person operation.

Rather than wallow in defeat, Sahil leaned into simplicity. He turned to AI tools to streamline operations—for example, predictive analytics to optimize pricing strategies for creators— and focused entirely on serving his community. Over the following years, Gumroad became a quiet juggernaut, generating millions in revenue with a single full-time employee: Sahil himself.

Today, Sahil speaks openly about the importance of balancing ambition with sustainability. He's crafted a business that fits his life, not the other way around. And by embracing constraints, he's found freedom.

The Biggest Lesson: Edit Ruthlessly

What can you subtract from your life—or your business—that isn't serving you? Sahil shows us that achieving success isn't always about scaling bigger; sometimes, it's about scaling smarter. Like a writer cutting unnecessary paragraphs, solo entrepreneurs must learn to edit their processes until only the essential remains.

Case Study 4: Rachel Woods – The AI Micromogul Reshaping Data Science

Rachel Woods once called herself "just an analytics geek," but today she's something much more than that: the founder of an AI empire. Armed with technical expertise and a sharp sense of market timing, Rachel built **The AI Exchange,** a one-stop shop for training professionals and businesses to harness AI tools effectively.

Initially, Rachel wore all the hats. She took phone calls, built the website, wrote content, and developed courses—all while experimenting with cutting-edge AI tools to automate repetitive tasks. ChatGPT created drafts of blog posts; MidJourney helped produce visuals. Slowly but surely, she created a business that looked far larger and more polished than it was, earning substantial revenue as word of mouth spread like wildfire.

What sets Rachel apart is her willingness to educate her audience—whether in-depth tutorials, accessible educational videos, or live workshops. People don't just turn to Rachel for AI strategy; they turn to her to learn how to think like her. In the process, she creates a community that constantly feeds growth back into her business.

The Biggest Lesson: Build Communities, Not Customers

Who are you helping? How can you deepen that relationship, so they don't just want your product but also want to grow alongside you? Rachel's success is proof that if you focus on creating value for a specific audience, profitability naturally follows.

The Common Threads

Across these stories, patterns emerge like breadcrumbs on a forest trail, guiding us toward the mindsets and tools that solo entrepreneurs must embrace to thrive:

1. **Execution Over Perfection:** None of these entrepreneurs waited until their ideas were flawless to launch. They iterated publicly, letting the world shape their products and services in real time.
2. **Automation as Leverage:** Without exception, they all used AI and automation tools to multiply their productivity. These tools—invisible to their users—freed them to focus on high-impact tasks.
3. **Authenticity and Alignment:** Each of these founders built businesses rooted in their unique passions and pain points. They are living proof that authenticity sells.
4. **Community at the Core:** Whether fostering digital nomads, content creators, or AI enthusiasts, they didn't just build businesses; they built tribes.

The Moment of Truth

Here's the question I'll leave you with, reader: **What's stopping you from being one of them?**

The tools they used are accessible to you. The mindset they adopted is yours for the taking. The only difference is that they started—and starting is always the hardest part. So, what idea have you been sitting on? What skill have you not yet unleashed on the world? What would happen if you took the leap today?

Remember, it isn't the size of the ship that determines the depth of the voyage—it's the courage of the captain. So go ahead. Set sail. The world is waiting.

CHAPTER 22

DIVERSITY IN AI
ENTREPRENEURSHIP

I n **The Grapes of Wrath**, John Steinbeck vividly described the
indomitable will of human beings to endure, adapt, and
ultimately triumph against overwhelming odds. His portraits of
characters like the Joad family remind us of one unshakable truth:
grit transcends social, economic, and geographical boundaries. As
I observe the rise of diverse leaders revolutionizing the field of
artificial intelligence, I cannot help but see parallels. AI, perhaps
the most transformative force of our time, isn't confined to Silicon
Valley offices or the minds of a singular demographic. It is being
shaped, refined, and weaponized for change by a chorus of voices
from every corner of the globe. The question is no longer whether
diversity matters in AI entrepreneurship—it is whether you, the
reader, recognize its full potential and your ability to be part of this
movement.

Today, the landscape of AI entrepreneurship looks far different
than it did during its genesis decades ago. Back then, it was fields
of sameness. From Palo Alto conference rooms to men's-only golf
foursomes, the architects of the AI revolution often came from
narrow bands of privilege. That is no longer the case. The
transformative power of AI entrepreneurship has found unlikely
adopters and champions. In this chapter, we'll explore stories of
innovation from underrepresented groups—stories that prove
artificial intelligence does not belong to a single demographic,
geography, or mindset. It belongs to all of us because humanity
itself is the great teacher of artificial intelligence.

As an aspiring or current entrepreneur in this space, I invite you to
pause and ask yourself: **Am I engaging with this technology as**

merely a tool, or as an equalizer? Because AI, by its very nature, is a mirror of the people who build it. If diverse individuals are driving the effort, then diversity becomes not just a buzzword, but a strategic advantage that is built into the DNA of AI itself.

The Global Shapers of AI

Let's begin with the story of M-Pesa, the mobile money platform that revolutionized banking in Kenya and throughout sub-Saharan Africa. Though not purely AI-driven at its inception, its successors have incorporated elements of AI to improve financial inclusion and create access to tools once reserved for the affluent. The next iteration of M-Pesa came in the form of Tala, started not in New York or London, but by Shivani Siroya, who grew up across three continents and was deeply familiar with the challenges communities in the developing world face. Tala uses machine learning to analyze smartphone data—texts, browsing behaviors, even keystroke intensity—to assess creditworthiness in areas where formal banking infrastructures are weak or non-existent. Today, Tala has issued billions of dollars in loans across global markets like Kenya, India, and the Philippines.

Shivani's story isn't about bringing AI to people; it's about enabling people to bring their stories, data, and challenges to AI. In doing so, she leveraged diversity not as a point of difference, but as her superpower. How many of us discount our own experiences because they seem unconventional? That question is where courage meets creativity: instead of asking **Do I belong here?**, ask: **What do I bring here that no one else does?**

Let's move now to Latin America, where an explosion of AI-powered startups is rewriting narratives. Take **NotCo**, a Chilean food tech company co-founded by Matías Muchnick, who partnered with data scientist Karim Pichara and biochemist Pablo Zamora. This unlikely trio created Giuseppe, an AI driven to develop plant-based substitutes for traditionally animal-based products. Raised in a geography often overlooked in both global tech and culinary innovation, they chose not to emulate Silicon Valley—they chose to embrace their roots and create what the world didn't have. Today, NotCo successfully competes with giants like Beyond Meat and Impossible Foods and has captured the imagination of both venture capitalists and Michelin-starred chefs.

Here's what I want you to note: diversity doesn't merely reflect the founder—it reflects the mission. NotCo wasn't just about business; it was a battle cry for sustainability, cultural identity, and looking at old problems through new lenses. Their diverse identities enabled them to focus not on what separates people, but on common human needs and aspirations.

If these stories tell us anything, it's this: when diversity is embraced in AI entrepreneurship, solutions often emerge not from what AI can automate or optimize, but from what it helps amplify—the values, creativity, and cultures of the world's population. Are you paying attention to the voices around you? Or are you leaning on the same frameworks that built yesterday's businesses?

Women in AI: Breaking Barriers, Defying Odds

The stats don't lie: women are severely underrepresented in technology, and AI is no exception. But new voices are disrupting the status quo. Meet Timnit Gebru, an Ethiopian-American computer scientist and former co-lead of Google's Ethical AI team. While she may not fall into the entrepreneurial class precisely, her work enables and influences entrepreneurs everywhere. Timnit has challenged longstanding narratives in AI development, from biases in facial recognition to the absence of ethical oversight in large-scale AI systems.

Inspired by her vision, entrepreneurs like Joy Buolamwini founded the Algorithmic Justice League to expose algorithmic bias. A Ghanaian-American computer scientist educated at MIT, Joy realized as an undergrad that the facial detection software she worked with recognized her face only when she donned a white mask. Her AI activism inspired entrepreneurial efforts worldwide around algorithmic fairness, proof that taking a stand against systemic flaws can itself become a springboard for innovation.

Are you aware of the biases you're building into your systems or the systems you're relying on? Are you asking the hard questions? People like Timnit and Joy remind us that entrepreneurship isn't just about creating—it's about **responsibility.**

Consider also the rise of entrepreneurial funds exclusively for women and creators of color. Melody Ehsani, who stepped into the wearables space by creating HERitage Watch with AI-enhanced design elements, explicitly centered her products around underrepresented communities. HERitage wasn't just about fashion or technology—it was about creating something those communities could feel authentically represented in.

How are you speaking to markets that have been ignored? What underserved groups are waiting, even willing to pay for, solutions only you can deliver authentically?

Collaboration as an Asset

In Zadie Smith's novel **White Teeth**, we watch as disparate families form connections against a backdrop of London's cultural chaos. The story is a reminder that diversity thrives in symbiosis—in collaboration. The same holds true for AI entrepreneurship. Diversity is about bringing multiple perspectives—not working in silos despite our differences, but because of them.

Consider H2Ok Innovations, co-founded by Anshuman Bapna and Erica Dawson. They joined forces to tackle water management issues using AI. What makes the company striking isn't just the problem it solves, but its DNA: a cross-cultural, cross-disciplinary partnership blending Erica's sustainability expertise with Anshuman's systems-thinking background. They didn't approach water as a technical issue—they approached it as a human one, where collaboration meant equity, access, and responsibility.

It's easy to see technology as a solitary pursuit, but again, I ask: who are you collaborating with? Are you seeking voices that challenge you, or are you choosing comfort?

The Big Takeaway: AI Is Human Intelligence

Ultimately, the rise of diversity in AI entrepreneurship isn't about altruism—it's about opportunity. It's about realizing the untapped wealth of ideas, perspectives, and markets sitting at the edges of our understanding. AI, for all its technological brilliance, is empty without us. It requires data, patterns, and—increasingly—ethical oversight. But above all, it requires innovation that speaks to the heart of humanity itself.

In Toni Morrison's **Song of Solomon**, there's a line about how knowing your own roots can give you the wings to fly. For AI entrepreneurship, the reverse is also true: it's by learning the roots of others—cultures, experiences, and geographies—that we unlock our full creative potential.

So here's the challenge I leave you with: What story are you telling with AI? Whose voices are being heard, and whose are being silenced? And above all, how will your own experiences—your unique upbringing, your challenges, your identity—become the competitive advantage you can bring to this space?

Diversity in AI entrepreneurship isn't just a moral imperative—it's a business one. And as history has shown us time and again, those who embrace inclusion are the ones who will endure, adapt, and ultimately, triumph. Will you?

CHAPTER 23

EARNING PASSIVE INCOME USING AI

I n his celebrated novel **The Great Gatsby**, F. Scott Fitzgerald romanticized the notion of wealth as a glimmering green light—a dream forever receding into the distance. And while Fitzgerald's characters pursued wealth through dubious means, you stand at the precipice of a more responsible, more accessible way to reach your own green light: using artificial intelligence to generate passive income. In this chapter, we will explore how AI can create lasting, scalable, and low-maintenance income streams, building not just wealth but freedom.

The promise of passive income has echoed through entrepreneurial circles for decades. It stirs the imagination, calling forth images of lounging on a beach while your capital works for you. But let me be clear: passive income is rarely truly passive— especially at the start. Building sustainable systems that allow for "hands-off" income requires sharp thinking, upfront effort, and precise execution. In today's world, the rise of generative AI systems, machine learning tools, and automation frameworks offers everyday entrepreneurs a powerful new set of tools to do just that.

This chapter is your blueprint. Together, let's look at three specific opportunities: creating automated e-commerce stores, taking advantage of generative content platforms, and building and licensing AI training datasets. Each avenue holds immense potential. The only question is: will you act?

The AI-Powered E-Commerce Revolution

In the early 2000s, the rise of websites like eBay and Shopify democratized entrepreneurship. Suddenly, anyone with a good idea could open an online store, bypassing barriers to entry like physical storefronts and massive inventory investments. Today, artificial intelligence has ushered in the second wave of e-commerce disruption—one that allows you to automate nearly every aspect of your store's operations, turning it into a near-passive source of income.

Example: The Dawn of AI Dropshipping

Consider Anna, a 34-year-old marketing specialist who, after losing her job during the pandemic, pivoted into running an AI-assisted dropshipping business. Anna used AI tools like ChatGPT to write compelling product descriptions, Jasper.AI to run targeted ad campaigns, and Oberlo (an e-commerce automation platform) to handle product sourcing and delivery.

With these tools, Anna identified a niche market—stylish, ergonomic desk accessories for remote workers. Once her products were listed, AI-enabled chatbots handled 90% of her customer service inquiries, while machine learning algorithms dynamically adjusted her pricing to ensure competitiveness. Within 12 months, Anna's store was generating $8,000 per month in passive income, requiring only an hour per week for maintenance.

The beauty of AI-driven e-commerce lies in its scalability. Today, even a one-person operation can emulate the efficiencies of a much larger company. Shopify recently integrated with tools like OpenAI and Tidio, allowing you to set up automated inventory tracking, email marketing, and customer personalization—all in one place. Do you see the potential here?

Key Takeaways for Your E-Commerce Pursuit

Here are four steps to create your first AI-powered passive income e-commerce store:

1. **Find a niche market**: Use tools like Google Trends and AnswerThePublic to identify underserved or trending markets. Pro tip: Try leveraging AI sentiment analysis tools (e.g., MonkeyLearn) to mine forums and social media for emerging consumer pain points.

2. **Automate your workflow**: Outsource tasks to AI tools like Re:Amaze for customer service, Pictory for quick video ad generation, and CJdropshipping for supply chain logistics.

3. **Let data guide your decisions**: By using AI analytics platforms like Klaviyo, you can track user behavior and micro-optimize your sales funnel—everything from ad click rates to abandoned cart recovery emails can be streamlined.

4. **Experiment with generative AI promotions**: Tools like Canva's AI feature allow you to whip up visually engaging promotions in minutes. Pair this with predictive targeting ads from Meta (formerly Facebook), and you can automate consistent traffic to your store.

Monetizing Generative Content Platforms

Imagine sitting under a tree, sketching out words onto a page, and discovering later that those words kept earning money long after you stepped away. This was the dream of American writers like Mark Twain, who prized royalties from his books as a form of passive income. Today, creative passive income is undergoing a renaissance thanks to AI—only now, the "authors" are machines.

Generative AI platforms like ChatGPT, MidJourney, and DALL·E are redefining what's possible in the realm of digital content. From writing e-books to producing stock images, these systems empower you to mass-produce intellectual property and monetize it through online distribution channels.

Example: Royalties 2.0—The Case of Steve, the AI Savvy Writer

Take Steve, for example. By day, Steve worked as a graphic designer. By night, he harnessed ChatGPT to co-write a series of short romance e-books under a pen name. Steve carefully outlined the story structure and used tools like NovelAI to enhance the narrative. For the book covers, he made creative use of MidJourney to generate visually striking designs that rivaled those of professional illustrators.

Steve uploaded his e-books to Amazon Kindle Direct Publishing (KDP). Within six months, he had 20 titles generating incremental sales. Each book took 5–7 hours to produce, and collectively, they now bring in $5,000 per month in royalties—with no additional input from Steve.

Let's zoom out for a moment. This strategy can be applied across multiple formats. You could compile recipe books with generative text tools, or even teach an online course filmed on a budget and then auto-captioned using Descript's AI transcription. These products require significant effort upfront, sure, but the potential recurring revenue could be life-changing.

Your Creative Launchpad

Ask yourself: What latent talents do you have that AI tools could amplify? Here are some AI-driven ideas to monetize generative content:

- AI-generated design prints for platforms like Redbubble or Society6.
- Self-publishing e-books or audiobooks on niche topics.
- Licensing music composed with AI platforms like AIVA for use in YouTube videos or advertisements.
- Building templates or digital planner content using tools like Canva and selling them on Etsy.

The Hidden Goldmine: AI Training Datasets

Somewhere in Silicon Valley, a product development team is hunched over a project that needs "training data" to build models that recognize, predict, or recommend effectively. Datasets are the lifeblood of artificial intelligence systems, and here's the kicker: someone, somewhere, is profiting from supplying them. Why not you?

While it's the least glamorous of our three strategies, licensing AI training datasets can be the most lucrative. When structured correctly, this is a true "set-it-and-forget-it" model. Companies, researchers, and institutions will pay top dollar for well-curated, unique repositories of data.

Example: The Story of Taylor's Image Dataset Empire

Taylor was a photographer with a knack for wildlife images, capturing rare birds and documenting unique animal behaviors. But instead of selling individual prints or licensing photos traditionally, Taylor chose a different route—she aggregated her work into datasets for training AI computer vision models.

Using platforms like Kaggle and Lionbridge, Taylor uploaded her datasets and licensed them to companies working on image recognition training. One contract alone netted her $30,000. Better still, she created an evergreen passive income stream by periodically updating and reselling her datasets to new clients.

Data doesn't need to come from photography alone. Imagine curating datasets in any niche that companies may want to train AI models in—product trend analysis, consumer sentiment logs, even language dialect databases.

Your Steps for Dataset Monetization

Here's how to get started:

1. **Choose your domain**: Think about areas where you either naturally have access to valuable data (e.g., industry connections) or where you can easily generate it (e.g., scraping public data).
2. **Organize and refine**: AI models thrive on clean, well-organized data. Tools like Labelbox and Amazon SageMaker allow you to annotate, enrich, and refine your datasets for better usability.
3. **Find buyers**: Platforms like Data Marketplace, Hugging Face, Lionbridge, and even AI research communities (via Reddit or Discord) are excellent for locating customers willing to pay for proprietary datasets.
4. **License, don't sell**: Don't undervalue your data by selling it outright. Licensing allows you to generate recurring revenue while retaining ownership.

Closing Thoughts: The Future Is AI-Infused Freedom

As you take a step back and look at these strategies, I challenge you to view passive income not as a distant dream but as an actionable reality. Each of these opportunities—be it AI-powered e-commerce, generative content royalties, or dataset licensing—requires effort upfront. But the reward isn't just money; it's freedom. AI can help you reclaim your time, expand your imagination, and walk a path not bound by a traditional 9-to-5 schedule.

Here's my challenge to you: Start with just one of these strategies over the next 30 days. Experiment. Test. Learn. The beauty of artificial intelligence is that it doesn't demand perfection; it simply requires a spark of action.

And someday, when your systems are humming along with minimal input from you, perhaps you'll remember the green light from **The Great Gatsby**. Only this time, it won't feel so far away.

CHAPTER 24

SCALING BY COLLABORATION: WHEN TO PARTNER AND WHEN TO AUTOMATE

There's a line in John Steinbeck's **Of Mice and Men** where Lennie, the well-meaning but misguided character, laments, "I got you to look after me, and you got me to look after you." While this is a story steeped in tragedy, this one sentiment touches on something profoundly universal: the power of collaboration. As solo founders navigating the Herculean task of building a business, we often ask ourselves: How much can I automate? How much should I do alone? And at what point does collaboration become not just beneficial, but essential?

The truth is, the journey of a solo entrepreneur is not always a solitary one. Yes, automation will help you move faster. It's the jet fuel for your rocket in a digitally-driven economy. But like any rocket, there comes a time when fuel alone will not suffice—you need air traffic control, a ground crew, and engineers to adjust your trajectory. The art of scaling lies in balancing these two forces: knowing when to lean into the efficiency of automation and recognizing when to partner with others to amplify your potential.

This chapter is your guide for navigating that balance. It will show you how to evaluate when you should double down on technology-enabled automation and when you should open the door to collaborators, partners, or even co-creators to take your venture to the next level.

Automation: Your First Scaling Partner

Before we delve into partnerships, let's acknowledge the rise of automation as the first and most scalable partner for any solo founder. There has never been a more opportune moment to delegate repetitive, low-value tasks to machines. From artificial intelligence tools like OpenAI's ChatGPT writing your marketing emails to Zapier integrating your workflows, automation enables you to squeeze more productivity out of every day. These tools act like invisible employees—impeccably efficient, surprisingly affordable, and immune to burnout.

Take, for example, Sara Blakely, the founder of Spanx. While known for her intense drive and creativity, even she recognized early on the importance of systems that could run without constant manual input. From automated email marketing flows to streamlined manufacturing processes, Spanx grew by leveraging technology to handle the "busy work," letting Sara focus on product innovation and customer-centric storytelling. Automation created a self-sustaining engine, enabling her company to scale exponentially faster than if she had tried to manage every detail herself.

But there's a trap in relying **too much** on automation. Like the unyielding machinery in Kurt Vonnegut's **Player Piano,** over-automation can strip a business of its humanity. When everything becomes a faceless system, you may struggle to create meaningful connections with customers or adapt dynamically to change. Automation doesn't innovate—it only implements. And that's where human relationships come into play.

The Ceiling of Automation: When Human Collaboration is Inevitable

Let me ask you a question: Can you automate spontaneity? Creativity? Trust?

Of course not. These are uniquely human traits, and they're often the very essence of what creates competitive advantage in a world drowning in perfectly functional systems. You can automate repetitive tasks, but you can't automate human ingenuity. And as your business grows, you will reach a point where scaling requires creating value that technology alone cannot deliver. That's where collaboration becomes your next growth strategy.

One way to identify the ceiling of automation is using the litmus test of complexity. If your business has complex needs involving cross-disciplinary expertise—like developing new technology, entering foreign markets, or scaling distribution—collaboration is no longer an optional luxury; it's a necessity. Imagine if Elon Musk had tried to scale Tesla or SpaceX as a solo operator, resisting collaboration in favor of automation. The sheer breadth of expertise—from engineering rocket propulsion systems to lobbying for better electric vehicle subsidies—required teams of world-class thinkers and executors. No amount of automation will write Tesla's master plan or build partnerships with NASA.

But collaboration doesn't always mean hiring a traditional team. As a solo founder building a unicorn enterprise, partnerships can take many forms: finding co-creators, outsourcing high-skill tasks, creating joint ventures, or collaborating with influencers who amplify your brand's reach.

Learning from Partnership in Action

Let's take a closer look at case studies that illustrate where collaboration has enabled businesses to scale far beyond their initial limitations.

1. Steve Jobs and Steve Wozniak (Apple Inc.)

One of the most iconic examples of scaling through partnership comes from a duo of founders who brought very different skills to the table: Steve Jobs and Steve Wozniak. On his own, Wozniak was a brilliant engineer capable of building revolutionary technology. But without Jobs' unique ability to envision a larger cultural narrative, foster key partnerships (like with investors and manufacturers), and scale Apple's operations, Woz's creations might have remained on the fringes of Silicon Valley.

As a solo founder, you might think you can embody both Jobs and Wozniak—but there is a cost to that approach. Jobs always recognized the power of leverage. His greatest collaboration wasn't just with Woz but with an ecosystem of partnerships: from PepsiCo's John Sculley to design legend Jony Ive.

The lesson? You don't have to be a jack-of-all-trades. Know when to look outside your immediate skill set to find collaborators who complement your strengths.

2. Oprah Winfrey and the Power of Collaboration Networks

Oprah Winfrey's career offers another powerful example of scaling through collaboration. While her magnetic personality and storytelling ability made her a billionaire, her empire was built through partnerships: from teaming up with publishing houses to elevate her book club to collaborating with other media brands on OWN (Oprah Winfrey Network). Oprah understood that leveraging other people's platforms and expertise allowed her to focus on what she did best: making meaningful emotional connections with her audience.

Can you identify partners who already have the distribution networks, credibility, or skill sets you lack? Instead of reinventing the wheel, what relationships could fast-forward your journey?

When NOT to Partner: Why Some Roads Are Meant to Be Walked Alone

It can be tempting to believe that every problem requires a collaborator. But partnerships come with costs. Collaboration requires negotiation, shared decision-making, and sometimes compromises that dilute your vision. That's not always the right answer for a solo founder trying to crystallize their unique offering.

Sometimes, the greatest progress happens when you resist collaboration. Author J.K. Rowling, for instance, famously wrote the Harry Potter series without a writing partner, focusing solely on her own creative vision. It was only after finishing her manuscripts that she sought collaborators in the form of publishers and editors. This approach of delayed collaboration allowed her to refine her ideas without external influence.

The decision to collaborate should also factor in how much control you're willing to give up. Many founders famously regret taking on the wrong partner or selling too much equity too early. As the author of this book, let me pose a critical question: Is this potential partnership a stepping stone—or a shackle? It's important to know the difference.

Building Your Collaboration Framework

Now that we've explored the principles, let's get practical. How do you decide whether a business need calls for automation or collaboration? Use this three-step framework as your blueprint:

1. Prioritize the Tasks You Hate or That Add No Unique Value:

Begin with delegation via automation. If a task is repetitive, low-skill, or unrelated to what makes your business indispensable, it's a prime candidate for automation. For example, consider automating customer support with chatbots or using project management software to streamline operations.

2. Identify Areas of Strategic Weakness:

Ask yourself: Where do I lack expertise? Are there areas where my progress has flatlined because I simply don't have the skills, resources, or network to move forward? These are prime opportunities to begin searching for collaborators. It might mean outsourcing specific tasks (like hiring a branding consultant) or forming deeper partnerships (like co-developing a new product line).

3. Consider Mutual Value in Every Partnership:

When considering collaboration, resist the temptation to ask, "What can I get?" Instead, ask, "What can I give that creates mutual benefit?" The strongest collaborations emerge when both parties feel like they're getting more from the alliance than they could achieve alone.

The Final Question: Are You Ready to Share the Story?

In **The Great Gatsby,** F. Scott Fitzgerald writes, "Can't repeat the past? Why of course you can!" This nostalgic lament reminds us of the human instinct to want to reclaim a single triumphant moment of control. But the reality of scaling a unicorn enterprise means letting others—whether it be code or collaborators—enter your story. It's a process of learning when to hold power close to your chest and when to share it, for shared power often grows exponentially.

So, back to you: Are you ready to scale by collaboration? What areas of your business are aching for human ingenuity, expertise, or empathy? And just as important, what areas can you automate so that your collaborations become focused and meaningful?

I leave you with this challenge: Over the next week, identify one task to automate and one area to explore a potential partnership. Dare to embrace both the inevitability of technology and the irreplaceable value of human connection. That's how a solo founder becomes a unicorn. That's how you go from good to great.

CHAPTER 25

THE FUTURE OF SOLOPRENEURSHIP IN THE AGE OF AI

I n Ernest Hemingway's **The Old Man and the Sea**, the protagonist, Santiago, is a solitary fisherman grappling with the vastness of the ocean, a force both unknowable and awe-inspiring. His tale is one of resilience, adaptation, and desperate mastery over nature. Today's solopreneurs — the lone founders, the one-person powerhouses — stand in their own boat, fishing for their future amidst the churning sea of artificial intelligence (AI). The question is: Will they seize the tools that AI provides to chart a course toward unimaginable success, or will they find themselves swept away by the tide?

This chapter is about that choice. It's about embracing AI not as a threat but as an extension of your abilities, a co-captain on your entrepreneurial journey. The solopreneurs of tomorrow will look very different from the industrious, time-strapped creators of the past. They will be amplified by machines but steered by human ingenuity. To stay ahead of this curve, to build your own single-handed unicorn enterprise in this new landscape, requires bravery, foresight, and a deep understanding of not only what AI can do, but also what it should do.

Welcome to solopreneurship in the age of AI — a brave new world where humans write the story but machines hold the pen.

Solopreneurship: A David Against the Corporate Goliaths

Before we dive into the future, let's first acknowledge how far solopreneurship has already come. Thirty years ago, the idea of competing as an individual against corporations with hundreds or thousands of employees would have seemed laughable. Imagine a single tailor trying to compete with Levi Strauss or an independent bookseller going head-to-head with Barnes & Noble.

But today, solopreneurs are everywhere — writers, creators, app developers, freelance consultants, and online education pioneers. With tools like Shopify, Substack, and Canva, the infrastructure has evolved to level the playing field and empower individuals to compete with large enterprises. Solopreneurs are no longer just Davids fighting corporate Goliaths; they are Davids armed with slingshots made of cutting-edge software.

And in the next evolution of this story, artificial intelligence is the ultimate force multiplier. It's not a slingshot anymore; it's the equivalent of turning Davids into Iron Man — human brilliance augmented by technological might. The question is not whether AI will change the way solopreneurs operate; the question is how you, as a forward-thinking solopreneur, can harness it to remain indispensable in a world where tech is ubiquitous but vision is rare.

AI as Your Competitive Advantage

Let's explore what's already happening. AI tools like Jasper and ChatGPT are making content creation faster and more accessible than ever before. Need a blog post about sustainable packaging options in under 30 seconds? Done. Need to translate it into five languages and adapt the tone for each cultural market? Easy. Tools like MidJourney enable solopreneurs to generate professional-grade visuals that used to require expensive designers. And let's not forget platforms like Bubble, where zero-coding entrepreneurs are creating fully functional apps without once touching a line of code.

Case in point: consider Emily, a fictionalized solopreneur based on the real-life creators I've met over the years. Emily is a career coach who used to spend countless hours writing LinkedIn posts to promote her services, designing slides for workshops, and managing her customer outreach. With AI tools, Emily now generates a week's worth of high-quality content in one afternoon. She uses ChatGPT for copy, Canva with AI design features for visuals, and even an AI CRM system to predictively suggest which of her prospects are closest to converting. Her productivity has tripled, and her revenue has doubled, all without hiring a team.

Think about that for a moment. Emily hasn't just automated tasks; she's elevated them. She's shifted time and energy from tactical execution to strategic thinking. She has rewired her business's focus from the microscopic to the telescopic.

Now ask yourself: How many time-draining, low-value tasks in your own business could you reimagine with AI? Are you holding on to processes that could be handled better, faster, or cheaper by a machine, simply because you're too attached to "how you've always done it"?

The Pitfall of Automation Without Intention

And yet, while this new reality promises infinite opportunity, it's not without its dangers. In Ray Bradbury's **Fahrenheit 451**, a society becomes so enamored with fast-paced, mechanized living that it loses its capacity for deep thought and introspection. The risk for solopreneurs in the age of AI is similar: in automating everything, you may begin to automate the things that make your business uniquely yours.

When you automate customer interactions, are you optimizing "efficiency" at the expense of empathy? When you let AI write your emails or design your graphics, are you letting your authentic voice become diluted? Machines may be fast, but they are lousy at storytelling. Stories are where connection happens; as a solopreneur, your ability to build that human connection is often your most valuable (and inimitable) asset.

When consulting with early-stage solopreneurs, I often ask: "What's the one thing only you can do?" For Emily, it was her ability to inspire her clients with personal, relatable anecdotes from her own career struggles. For another solopreneur, Michael, it was his knack for weaving humor into technical content about cybersecurity — a niche, but utterly human, skill.

AI can do a lot of magical things, but it cannot be you. Your creativity, your empathy, your vision — these are the elements that will allow you to rise above the noise of automation. So, collaborate with the machines, by all means, but never forget who's steering the ship.

Future Trends: What's on the Horizon?

The age of AI is just getting started. Let's explore key trends that all solopreneurs should anticipate:

1. AI-Enhanced Niching

AI will empower solopreneurs to specialize in increasingly narrow niches and serve smaller, more customized markets. Where once you might have aimed to be a "freelance graphic designer," now you can become "the world's leading expert on time-lapse animation for e-commerce brands." With AI tools, you can create expertise rapidly, and your reputation can precede you at a global scale. Micro-niches will thrive.

2. The Rise of Personal AI Assistants

Rather than using a hodgepodge of AI tools, solopreneurs will begin deploying personal AI assistants — think of them as "Chief of Staff AI" software tailor-made to their business. This concierge-level software will learn your specific habits, preferences, and even your industry audience, customizing its advice and outputs. Imagine scheduling, customer support, marketing, and financial forecasting all delegated to a single AI co-pilot.

3. Hyper-Transparency and Authenticity as Differentiators

As AI-generated content floods the market, audiences will crave transparency and authenticity. They will want to know who is behind the curtain. This provides a massive opportunity for solopreneurs who are willing to "show their work" and provide a human touch. Explain to your customers, "This was written by me, with a little help from AI." Transparency will become a trust-building superpower.

4. AI Legislation and Ethics Will Matter

Governments and institutions are catching up to the implications of widespread AI use. Expect stricter regulations around privacy, data usage, and disclosure of AI-produced work. Solopreneurs who develop a clear ethical stance on how they're deploying AI will earn respect and loyalty — staying ahead of the curve rather than reacting to it.

The Big Question: What Kind of Solopreneur Will You Become?

There are two types of stories unfolding here. On one side, there's the solopreneur who embraces AI blindly, becoming fully mechanized, generic, and replaceable. This is the character who stands in front of the ocean of AI, paralytic, waiting to be overtaken by the waves. On the other side is the solopreneur who uses AI intentionally, pairing the power of technology with the richness of their creative and human insights. This character uses AI as an oar, not as a boat.

Which character will you become?

Will you automate for efficiency at the cost of originality? Or will you strategically use automation to free up the time and energy to become more human in your work?

Closing Thoughts: The Art of the Possible

Returning to Hemingway's Santiago, he may have been alone on the water, but he was never really alone. He had his instincts, his intelligence, his years of experience. And those were his true companions, guiding his journey through hardship and triumph.

As a solopreneur in the age of AI, you too are never really alone. You have endless tools, models, and possibilities at your fingertips. But more importantly, you have the one thing no algorithm can replicate: yourself. The heart, the vision, and the humanity three steps ahead of the machine.

Your future is the fusion of technology and humanity. And the story you write will be the one no AI could ever tell.

So, set your sights on the horizon. The ocean is vast, but your potential is greater.

CHAPTER 26

LOSING THE FEAR OF FAILURE: EXPERIMENTATION IN AI BUSINESSES

ailure. The word itself seems to reverberate in our minds with an almost physical weight. It's a sharp-edged echo of every rejected idea, every public misstep, every late-night worry. But what if I told you that the fear of failure is the heaviest barrier keeping you from making progress? What if, instead of seeing failure as a stop sign, you viewed it as a necessary ingredient for success, particularly in the world of AI entrepreneurship—a rocky but exhilarating frontier defined by constant iteration, uncertainty, and adaptability?

In this chapter, I want to challenge you to think of failure not as an abyss but as a staircase. Missteps are part of the climb. And for solo founders navigating the intricate pathways of AI, losing the fear of failure means embracing experimentation with courage, resilience, and a clear vision. Let's unpack how.

Experimentation in a World of Uncertainty

In the realm of building a solo-led AI business, risk isn't just part of the equation—it **is** the equation. If you're not experimenting, you're not innovating. And if you're not innovating in the rapidly shifting AI space, you're falling behind. Unlike traditional business paradigms where outcomes might be predictable to a certain degree, AI thrives in an ambiguous, chaotic, and astonishingly dynamic environment. Data changes. Algorithms shift. Markets evolve. If you demand perfect clarity before you act, you've already missed the moment.

Consider the lead-up to GPT-based chat platforms becoming mainstream. When OpenAI first unveiled their generative models, even they couldn't predict the exact applications or impact these systems would have. Yet they didn't wait for complete answers. They iterated, tested, failed, and adjusted. This experimental approach allowed them to gradually refine their offerings. Similarly, as a solo AI founder, you need to test, fail, learn, and repeat—fast.

Edwin Land, the co-founder of Polaroid, famously said, "A mistake is an event, the full benefit of which has not yet been turned to your advantage." In the AI space, mistakes aren't setbacks; they're signals. They guide you toward what works. But how do you avoid treading into reckless experimentation? By learning to quantify risks and iterate intelligently.

Quantifying Risk: Setting Guardrails for Experimentation

Experimentation does not mean plunging blindly into uncertainty. If you're building a solo AI startup, you don't have room for reckless leaps. Every step you take matters, because every decision you make commands not just your time and resources, but your energy—and possibly your survival.

Imagine you're crossing a canyon on a rickety suspension bridge. Every board creaks and every gust of wind shakes your balance. You don't charge forward blindly, yet you don't linger, paralyzed by fear. Instead, you calculate. You determine where you can step confidently, and which points demand additional caution.

In AI businesses, this deliberate calculation manifests as establishing **minimum viable experiments (MVEs)**—low-cost, easily testable iterations of your ideas. Think of Zara, the fast-fashion giant that disrupted a vast industry. They don't guess at what trends will resonate. They use small batches—tiny "experiments"—to send items to select stores and measure customer response before scaling up production. You can use this same principle in your AI venture by deploying small-scale prototypes or proofs of concept before investing full-on.

Here's an example: Imagine you're building an AI recommendation engine for DIY home renovators. Instead of plunging headfirst into designing the full product, you might run an MVE by asking users to input a few preferences and generating a list of basic suggestions manually. If the basic idea resonates, you can start automating parts of the process, using data from that first test as your guide.

Ask yourself: What's the smallest, simplest version of my idea that I can release into the wild? Where is the line between smart risk and overcommitment? When you've identified that, you're ready to iterate intelligently.

Iterating Intelligently: Learning from Data, Not Emotions

The essence of successful entrepreneurship is iteration—not just doing it over and over but doing it better each time. Solo founders often have the burden (and luxury) of wearing every hat: product designer, marketer, data analyst, customer support agent. This makes iteration an intensely personal process, but it's **data**, not emotion, that should guide your path forward.

Take Netflix. In its early days, Netflix wasn't a streaming provider. It was a DVD rental service, shipping discs to customers via mail. They didn't immediately become the entertainment giant we know today, but what set them apart was how they iterated. Netflix relied heavily on its customer data to determine what was working, and when they discovered that people were leaving DVDs in their envelopes for weeks at a time before even watching them, they proposed something audacious: What if customers didn't have to wait for physical content? This inspired their transformation into a streaming platform—and then, into a content creator.

The same principle applies to your AI business. Whether you're teaching a machine to understand natural language or predict supply chain disruptions, you must let client and system data inform your decisions. For instance:

1. What metrics validate your progress? Is it engagement, accuracy, or scalability?

2. Instead of merely seeking validation for your hypotheses (confirmation bias is a founder's greatest weakness), are you actively searching for opportunities to disprove assumptions so you can refine your approach?

3. What does the "failure" of your prototype really mean? Is it a design flaw, a marketing gap, or a system limitation?

When you listen to the data, you take emotions out of the equation. And when ego doesn't cloud your decision-making, you iterate with clarity and objectivity.

Bouncing Back: The Phoenix Phenomenon

Failure isn't the opposite of success. It's part of the process. To lose the fear of failure is to acknowledge that setbacks are inevitable— and that resilience is your superpower. The question isn't **if** something will go wrong but how you'll respond when it does.

I think of J.K. Rowling and her journey to publishing **Harry Potter**. It wasn't just a story of rejection; it was a story of endurance. Twelve publishers turned her down before one took a chance on her manuscript. And today, that manuscript has built an entire universe of books, movies, merchandise, and theme parks. Rowling's story reminds us that resilience stems from the belief in our end goal, no matter how many times we hear "no."

So, what does bouncing back look like as an AI entrepreneur? It means reframing every failed experiment as a lesson, then re-entering the game with sharper insights. Consider Andrew Ng, co-founder of Google Brain. When Google Brain's early work on speech recognition consistently hit roadblocks, rather than scrapping the project, Ng's team dug deep into understanding their failures. They realized that overcoming their acoustic modeling challenges required neural networks with significantly more computational power—and they set about building it.

Bouncing back doesn't just build your product; it builds **you**. Each setback strengthens your adaptability, deepens your understanding of your field, and trains you to approach obstacles with creativity. But resilience isn't just a mindset—it's a muscle.

You strengthen it by embracing discomfort, repeatedly venturing into the unknown, and taking ownership of your journey.

Changing the Relationship: What If Failure is Not Personal?

Fear of failure often stems from one misconception: That failure defines **you**. It doesn't. Failure isn't personal—it's a function of testing what works. If Edison had associated every failed filament experiment with his self-worth, the light bulb might never have been born.

Let me pose a question to you: Are you conflating the outcomes of your experiments with your identity as a founder? If an algorithm you built doesn't meet expectations, does it mean you're bad at your job—or that your ideas need more iteration? Shifting your mindset from a fear-based, ego-driven perspective to one rooted in learning and curiosity is one of the most liberating gifts you can give yourself as a solo founder.

In Ryan Holiday's book **The Obstacle Is the Way**, he pulls from Roman stoicism to argue that adversity isn't just a hindrance—it's the way forward. The same is true of failure. Each setback is a classroom. Each mistake is a breadcrumb on the trail. Follow them.

Closing Questions: Challenge Yourself

As we close this chapter, I want you to reflect deeply on your current relationship with failure and experimentation. I'll leave you with a set of questions that will help you assess your readiness to lose the fear of failure and scale your AI business to staggering heights:

1. What experiment can you run this week that, if it fails, would still teach you something valuable about your business?
2. How could you break down an aspect of your business into smaller parts to test and iterate more quickly?
3. When you've experienced setbacks in the past, did you spend more time analyzing what went wrong or worrying about what others might think? What can you let go of?

4. How much time are you spending in the planning stage?
    And when will you decide it's time to take action,
    regardless of your fear?

In the vast, uncharted territory of AI entrepreneurship, there are
no absolute answers, but there is a compass. Failure is not the final
chapter. It's merely a plot twist in your story. Welcome it. Learn
from it. Then chart your next course. Because every AI unicorn—
yes, even the ones you admire—was built not by avoiding failure
but by dancing with it.

CHAPTER 27

THE NETWORK EFFECT
FOR SOLO ENTREPRENEURS

A cold winter night. A young entrepreneur sits in their home office, staring at a blank digital canvas on their laptop. Their head swirls with ideas—a revolutionary AI app, an online product for global audiences—but a sobering thought weighs heavy: **How do I compete with giants like Google or Meta with just myself?**

The answer, dear reader, lies in a concept as ancient as markets themselves but made newly potent in the digital world: the network effect.

In William Faulkner's classic **Light in August**, he writes about how people are "neither entirely gods nor animals but something in between." One could say the same about ideas. Alone, a great idea is a seed, fragile and isolated. But planted in fertile soil, with networks crisscrossing like mycorrhizal fungi within the earth, that seed grows into something world-shaking. For the solo entrepreneur, building and leveraging network effects represents the cathedral under which your single-player idea can bloom into a billion-dollar venture. Your unicorn.

Let's get practical. In this chapter, you'll learn what the network effect is, why it matters, and, most importantly, how to wield it like a practiced craftsperson, even if you're a solo operator. No gigantic team. No astronomical venture capital. Just you, your creativity, and a carefully nurtured community.

The Power of the Network Effect: A Brief Refresher

First, let's get clear on what the network effect actually is. In its simplest form, the network effect means that the value of a product or platform increases as more people use it. The textbook examples include Facebook and LinkedIn—platforms that become exponentially more viable as their user base grows. If you're the only one with a telephone, it's useless; but as soon as a network of people own telephones, each additional user amplifies its utility for everyone else.

But here's the nuance: this isn't just for social networks or tech giants. The network effect can be harnessed for micro-communities, niche audiences, and community-driven startups. For a solo entrepreneur, the point isn't to be Facebook—it's to create your **own small, scalable ecosystem,** one that feeds off itself and creates compounding returns.

The real magic of the network effect? Once it begins, **it scales without your intervention.** That's how you, the solo entrepreneur, turn hours into exponential results. It's a force multiplier, a bit like releasing a river after building a meticulous system of dams and channels. At first, you must craft and nurture, deeply and patiently. But when done correctly? The river runs itself.

Step One: Build a Community Before You Build a Product

Remember, network effects only work when you have a **network**. The foundation isn't in the lines of code you write or the algorithms you develop—it's in the people you gather around your vision.

Think of Wattpad, the storytelling platform. Allen Lau, its founder, started with a simple observation: storytelling is inherently social. But early on, instead of investing all resources in the perfect product, Wattpad focused on creating **a community of readers and writers**. Lau nurtured this community, actively engaging with early adopters, soliciting feedback, and amplifying success stories within the group. The platform's value, of course, grew in tandem with its users: writers attracted readers, readers promoted the stories they loved, and the viral loop began turning.

You don't need millions of users on Day One to replicate this framework. As a solo entrepreneur, start small. Identify an underserved but passionate niche. Who are your "early believers"? These people are your co-authors—they'll help you build your first prototype, refine your messaging, and spread the word.

Take, for instance, a hypothetical AI-driven journaling app with a focus on mindfulness (let's call it **MindNet**). Instead of rushing your app to market, imagine starting with a tight-knit community of 500 meditation enthusiasts on Reddit or Discord. Engage with them; host Q&A chats, share prototypes, and co-create features with them. Invite them into your journey.

Challenging question: Who is your ideal niche? What specific group would be **delighted** to share your mission? Have you reached out to them yet—or are you locked in solitary creation mode?

Step Two: Build Interactions, Not Just Features

Now that you've envisioned a community-centric launch, it's time to design around interaction. This is where solo entrepreneurs often stumble. Their first instinct is to pack their product with features, assuming utility alone will attract users. Wrong. The foundation of the network effect lies in **how and why people interact** with your platform.

Consider OpenAI's ChatGPT, which exploded in popularity in late 2022. Part of its genius wasn't just the AI itself—it was the ecosystem of interactions it enabled. Some users generated funny quizzes and educational resources; others built scripts or solved coding problems collaboratively. The product wasn't just the AI— it was how millions of users reshaped their workflows and shared use cases with each other. The fundamental question is: **How does each user benefit when they see someone else using what you've created?**

For our hypothetical **MindNet** journaling app, let's apply this lesson. Your app isn't just a glorified notepad. It's a space where users may exchange mindfulness tips, read anonymized passages from other users to inspire their own reflection, or even participate in daily community topics. You're building connections on top of systems.

The long-term battle isn't won by chasing a better feature, but by crafting structures that encourage more and more meaningful participation. Here's a test: If you vanished tomorrow, would your product's community keep interacting with each other? If yes, you're on the right track.

Step Three: Incentivize Sharing Without Becoming Spammy

One of the golden levers for solo entrepreneurs is figuring out how to supercharge the viral loop **ethically**. The secret to scaling network effects is getting users to bring in other users, but not in a way that feels coercive or annoying. If the only reason people share your product is because they're bribed (think shady referral codes), your network is brittle. Instead, you want sincere, intrinsic advocacy.

Dropbox nailed it. Solo-founder Drew Houston launched Dropbox at a time when countless other cloud-storage competitors existed. What changed the game was its referral program: users weren't just rewarded for signing others up—they were offered free storage space, something directly beneficial within the product. Every referral made the advocate's experience richer, and they became a walking billboard for Dropbox in their social circles. The result? Exponential growth—one friend converting another, then hundreds more.

Returning to our example app **MindNet**, instead of generic invites, empower users to share something meaningful tied to the app, like a "Mindfulness Challenge" or a new insight their journaling unlocked. If sharing brings tangible benefit (more so than gamified points or empty kudos), users will do it naturally.

Challenging question: Can you name three ways your users are **excited** to talk about your product? Would they share it gladly, or would they hesitate because it feels awkwardly transactional?

Step Four: Plug Into Stronger Networks

If you've read this far, you know my philosophy: solo entrepreneurship doesn't mean going it alone. With savvy execution, you can stand on the shoulders of existing giants, leveraging **their** networks to turbocharge your own growth.

Think about how the single developer behind the game **Flappy Bird**, Dong Nguyen, found success in 2013. His simple app went viral not because he promoted it widely himself but because he launched it on prebuilt app-network platforms like Apple's App Store, where millions of users were already hunting for their next time-killer game. These networked environments acted as amplifiers for his reach.

Or consider indie AI developers today leveraging API ecosystems like OpenAI or Hugging Face. By layering micro-apps on top of world-class AI engines, they instantly access a ready-made network of users and developers eager to build collaboratively.

For **MindNet**, this may mean integrating your journaling insights directly into Slack, Discord, or email—whichever "network stream" your target audience lives in already. Why swim against stronger tides?

Step Five: Scale Without Losing Soul

Growth is intoxicating. But it's also risky, particularly when solo entrepreneurs forget the community that willed their success into existence.

Peloton represents a cautionary tale here. What began as a fervently engaged fitness community spiraled into troubled waters once it shifted its focus almost entirely to high-end subscribers and neglected grassroots evangelists. The brand's perceived exclusivity alienated original users who had invested years in making the community vibrant. Success, ironically, made it vulnerable.

Take a cue from a different field. Duolingo, started by a small team but eventually helmed by its founder Luis von Ahn, has scaled its platform while doubling down on its fun, quirky community. By encouraging goofy leaderboards and memes (who hasn't seen jokes about Duo the Owl stalking them?), Duolingo grew its network effects—without abandoning its scrappy origins.

Ask this now: If your product hit 1 million users tomorrow, how would you keep your **Day One users** engaged and loved? The product may scale, but your humanity must scale with it.

Closing Challenge: Planting Your Forest

In the American classic **The Overstory** by Richard Powers, trees tell intergenerational tales, their forests serving as ecosystems of interconnected life. The moral? A solo tree may thrive, but a forest can endure storms, fires, even centuries of change.

My question for you: What forest are you planting with your solo business? Which connections will grow naturally, even organically, long after your initial effort? You aren't just building a product—you're building an ecosystem, symbiotic, vibrant, and alive.

That's your challenge—to harness network effects and create value that grows **on its own**. Take your seed, plant it well, and watch it reshape the soil beneath your feet. One user. Then two. Then two million.

That is how you—one person, one dream—can launch your unicorn.

CHAPTER 28

THRIVING IN SATURATED INDUSTRIES WITH AI DIFFERENTIATION

The tech boom brought us into an era of hyper-saturation. Whether you're in food and beverage, real estate, healthcare, or e-commerce, chances are your market is teeming with comparable businesses clawing for the same customer dollar. This might feel like a dog-eat-dog world, but here's the twist: Your "farm" doesn't have to run out of soil or water. Instead, by deploying AI strategically, you can leverage untapped opportunities where others see nothing but constraints. AI isn't just a tool; it's a compass that guides you to fertile ground. In this chapter, we decode the art of differentiation in saturated industries and explore how the marriage of creativity and artificial intelligence can turn even the most cutthroat, oversaturated playing fields into fertile niches for your singular unicorn enterprise.

The Big Problem with "The Same"

In his novel "The Road," Cormac McCarthy portrays a bleak world of scarcity where survival hinges on standing apart, often with brutal consequences. Ironically, entrepreneurs in saturated markets face a similar stark reality. Imagine a bustling farmer's market with ten vendors selling the exact same apple pie. The only difference? Who yells the loudest. That's often what saturation feels like—shouting into an ocean of noise, hoping for your voice to carry through the din.

Here's the bad news: Shouting louder is a losing strategy. Discounts, incremental feature changes, or minor branding upgrades won't cut it in today's hypercompetitive landscape. But here's the good news: Artificial intelligence carves new roads where none existed. It lets you **outthink** and **outcreate** your competition rather than just outspend or outrun them. AI can be the precise brushstroke that differentiates your enterprise's portrait from the gallery of sameness.

But first, consider this: How many businesses fail because the owners copy competitors blindly rather than excavate for true innovation? Which are you—part of the flock, or the person designing the map?

Redefining Differentiation: Inspiration from Tesla and Netflix

Differentiation is not a new concept for unicorn enterprises. Tales of Tesla and Netflix provide key lessons when mapped to AI. Tesla didn't reimagine the steering wheel or emblazon it with flashier logos—they rebuilt the car from its bones up. Netflix didn't simply negotiate better deals with studios; it pivoted into predictive algorithms that shaped cultural trends rather than reacting to them.

AI offers the same potential for profound differentiation. The key lies in moving past improving what exists and into rethinking the very DNA of your process, strategy, or customer experience within your industry.

Take Tesla: Its usage of AI in autonomous driving systems isn't just a feature—it redefines what it means to own and use a car. The same principle applies to Netflix. Its AI recommendation engine doesn't merely suggest "what to watch next"; it actively curates content that mesmerizes customers and keeps them subscribed for years. In both cases, AI is not an accessory; it's the **core differentiator**.

Your Challenge: What could be the Tesla of **your** industry? What part of your value chain can AI fundamentally rewrite?

Step 1: Diagnose the Saturation Problem

To differentiate in a saturated market, you first need to understand it. What makes a market saturated isn't just quantity—it's the redundancy of offering. For instance, there are countless coffee shops, but Starbucks differentiates itself with its personalization ecosystem, much of which is AI-powered. From an app that tailors recommendations based on buying habits to real-time inventory adjustments, Starbucks is playing a different game entirely.

Let's start with your business. Ask yourself:

1. **What are your competitors not solving for?** Saturated industries often mirror each other. That's your opportunity. What blind spots exist because everyone assumes the same things?
2. **Where are the inefficiencies?** Saturated markets often bog down under their own weight. Are competitors wasting time, resources, or opportunity that AI could optimize?

Imagine you're selling shoes. The saturated response would be, "We've got this style on sale!" Here's a differentiated response: "We use AI-driven foot scanning technology to create a shoe that fits like a glove—and predict when you'll need a replacement." The former fights for attention; the latter carves a niche.

Case Study: Stitch Fix and the Art of Hyper-Personalization

Stitch Fix entered the saturated world of fashion retail with a promise to personalize style. Competitors like department stores and online retailers had access to catalogs ten times larger than Stitch Fix's lineup. But instead of fighting on scale, Stitch Fix deployed AI to solve a unique problem: aligning consumer preferences efficiently with curated choices.

Here's how: Its algorithms analyze user data—style quizzes, past purchases, return reasons—and cross-reference these insights with inventory trends and stylist expertise. The outcome is a genuinely unique shopping experience where the customer feels seen, understood, and celebrated. Stitch Fix thrived by answering a simple question: Can AI make customers feel like there's a stylist dedicated **just to them**?

What "personalization gap" could AI tackle in **your** business?

Step 2: Turn AI Into a Problem-Solving Weapon

One of AI's greatest strengths is its ability to process massive amounts of data and deliver surprising insights. This is where innovation for differentiation is born.

Example 1: Lemonade Insurance—Simplifying a Complex Industry

The insurance industry is perhaps one of the most saturated and misunderstood spaces imaginable. Yet Lemonade used AI to differentiate. Its secret? Speed and transparency. By using AI-powered chatbots to expedite claims processing and new customer onboarding, Lemonade promises an insurance experience that feels more human (ironically enough) than traditional companies offering paper-pushing processes.

Not only did Lemonade streamline one of the industry's main bottlenecks, but it also used AI to align its brand values with its social mission. Its AI helps route profits from unused premiums toward nonprofits chosen by their customers. What other insurance company does that?

Now reflect: What bottlenecks plague your industry? Could AI both speed them up and simultaneously underscore the values of your brand?

Example 2: Peloton—Data as Community Power

Markets like fitness equipment are riddled with options—all promising the convenience and flexibility of working out at home. Peloton broke through the noise by using AI to create a **community-driven fitness ecosystem** rather than just selling a stationary bike.

Peloton's algorithms don't merely recommend workouts—they craft personalized playlists, predict coaching styles users prefer, and even tap into social features (e.g., real-time leaderboard rankings). This combination fosters a sense of emotional and social investment in users. The more riders engage, the stronger their bond with the Peloton brand. AI wasn't just an add-on; it served as connective tissue, uniting data and emotional resonance.

What tools exist in your industry that could be transformed from commodities into emotional connectors using AI? How can you deepen relationships or create loyalty ecosystems?

Step 3: Aim for "Super-Niche Dominance"

In "The Great Gatsby," Fitzgerald describes the "orgastic future" that eludes most dreamers—always visible but tantalizingly out of reach. For readers of this book, your goal isn't global, instant dominance; it's a laser-focused **super-niche** where you can dominate unequivocally. AI allows you to peel back the layers of your audience with precision so that you can hyper-focus on one task, product, or demographic.

Case Study: Grammarly's AI-Powered Prose for Professionals

Think about grammar-checking software: It's as dull a market as it gets. Yet Grammarly transformed its product into a near-mandatory tool for writers, students, and corporate professionals. How? AI-driven editing not only corrected grammar errors but also analyzed tone, clarity, formality, and audience intent.

Grammarly didn't name itself king of all communication tools—it niched down to "helping anyone write better instantly." That super-niche eventually scaled upward into partnerships with LexusNexus for law firms, integrations into Microsoft Word suites, and more. Rather than competing with the broad, crowded market of educational tools, it built credibility one focused audience segment at a time.

Step 4: Marry Data with Story

AI delivers differentiation most effectively when it helps customers feel a deeper connection with a brand. And here's the paradoxical truth about AI: The more it optimizes systems and decision-making, the more room humans have to focus on emotion and storytelling—two things AI cannot replicate.

Brands like Airbnb have been leveraging this duality. Airbnb's AI-powered dynamic pricing engine maximizes listings and guest bookings, but its storytelling—personal homes, unique experiences—is what makes customers loyal. AI takes care of the complexity so humans can focus on emotion.

Ask yourself this: If AI could optimize all your operational headaches, what story would you be freed up to tell? What aspect of your brand's emotional connection to customers could you amplify? Ultimately, data creates trust, but stories inspire loyalty.

Closing Challenge: Forget the Competition

In "To Kill a Mockingbird," Harper Lee's Atticus Finch reminds us: "You never really understand a person until you consider things from their point of view." In entrepreneurship, the same holds true for the customer. AI gives you the tools to understand your customer better than your competitors ever could. When used effectively, AI allows you to stop chasing competitors altogether because you've established a realm that only **you** understand and occupy.

Here's the ultimate question I leave you with:

What niche can you own so completely, so irreplaceably, that the concept of competition doesn't matter anymore? How will you leverage AI not just to survive—but to thrive?

The answers rest not in mimicking what others have done but in using AI to create what doesn't yet exist. Saturation is not a dead end; it's a challenge for true creators, true innovators, and true world-builders to rise. Will you take up that challenge?

CHAPTER 29

MINDSET MASTERY FOR SOLO UNICORN BUILDERS

uilding a billion-dollar business as a single founder — a solo unicorn — is not for the faint of heart. Let's dispel the romance of it up front: this is not a swashbuckling, cinematic montage where one good idea leads to overnight success and drives you to stand on the TED stage. It's more akin to Steinbeck's depiction of the relentless dust storms in **The Grapes of Wrath**—a grinding, unglamorous battle against adversity, external challenges, and the ever-present voice in your head questioning if you've got what it takes.

The solo entrepreneur's journey is one of paradoxical solitude. You're steering the ship alone, but unlike Odysseus in **The Odyssey**, there's no mythical crew around you to help when the sirens call. There's just you and your mental armor. And here's a fundamental truth: while business success takes creativity, market acumen, and yes, technical skills, sustainable success demands an unshakable mindset first and foremost. A mindset that doesn't just weather storms but thrives in their midst.

This chapter is your roadmap to mental mastery because no unicorn is built without the mind of an entrepreneur who already believes it's possible.

1. The Groundwork: The Power of Decision, Not Desire

Warren Buffett famously said, "The chains of habit are too light to be felt until they are too heavy to be broken." Your mindset is not formed in a day, but rather in the micro-decisions you stack, consciously or unconsciously, each day. To build a solo unicorn, you need to invest daily in the habits that fortify your psychology.

Think about Sara Blakely, the solo founder of SPANX. In interviews, Blakely emphasizes how her decisions—not her product ideas—carried her through the early days. She rewired her self-perception by embarking on what she called a "mental marathon," embracing failure as data rather than defeat, and consciously reframing rejection as a stepping stone. Did she desire success? Sure. But it was her decision to harness failure differently that set the foundation for her meteoric rise.

The Lesson: Desires are fleeting; decisions are foundational. Desire whispers, "I want this." Decision declares unapologetically, "I'm willing to do whatever it takes." As a solo unicorn builder, adopt Sara's mental marathon approach: write down **one decision** every day that aligns your actions with your ultimate vision.

2. Mental Models: Think in Systems, Not Sprints

Let's carve one major distinction right here: solo unicorn builders don't think in outputs; they think in systems. Why? Because systems prevent the mental whiplash of short-term gratification. Elon Musk, solo founder of everything from Zip2 to SpaceX (in their respective infancies), designed mental frameworks that operate in decades, not deadlines. Musk often references his reliance on **first principles thinking** — the practice of distilling every problem to its fundamental truths and reasoning up from there.

Here's how it works in practical terms: Suppose you're overwhelmed with the thought, "I don't have the budget for this product launch." Instead of spiraling, break the situation into its most elemental parts:

- What is the smallest functional version of the launch I can test right now?
- What assumptions are driving my fear, and how can I verify or disprove them?
- What systems could I create to automate or simplify the process for future launches?

Mental models like these keep you from being paralyzed by the enormity of the unicorn dream and instead help you operate in manageable steps. Think about the railroad in Ayn Rand's **Atlas Shrugged**: each track was only one part of the puzzle for the transcontinental vision. Similarly, each decision you make becomes a system that connects the dots.

The Lesson: Think long-term, but execute in systems. Build scaffolding in your mind—a series of interconnected strategies and safeguards—so you focus on leverage, not just brute force.

3. The Emotional Contingency Plan: Preparing for Failure Without Succumbing to It

Let me ask you this: When your next product idea flops, or when sales trickle in slower than expected, how will you respond? Denial? Panic? Let's revisit Blakely. She shares a story of how, when pitching her now-famous product SPANX to department store after department store, she heard "no" 99% of the time. Her father had conditioned her to frame rejection differently: "What did you fail at today?" he'd ask her every evening growing up. Failure wasn't shameful in their household; it was encouraged, even celebrated.

Contrast this with the "shame-based avoidance" many first-time entrepreneurs experience. Instead of seeing failure as a stepping stone, they conflate it with personal inadequacy. How quickly would you stop running if, every time you tripped, you declared walking itself a doomed enterprise?

As a solo founder, you need an emotional contingency plan—a way of ensuring that failure doesn't derail your mindset. Start by conducting a deliberate mental exercise:

-   **Write this down right now:** "If my next launch doesn't work out, I will..."
-   Create **three actionable recovery steps** you'd take to pivot, reassess, or improve.

You're not bracing for failure to invite it; you're doing so to neutralize its power over you.

The Lesson: Failure isn't the opposite of success; it's tuition. Prepare for it with a blueprint, so when it happens, you act instead of react.

4. Burnout Immunity: The Art of Governing Your Machine

Many solo unicorn builders approach work like marathoners sprinting the first mile. The problem is, martyrdom to productivity is the fastest route to burnout. Jeff Bezos, for all the superhero narratives around Amazon's creation, famously advocates an opposite approach: making "a small number of high-quality decisions" a day. Bezos understands what most people miss—your brain is a battery, not a bottomless well.

If you're filling your calendar with meetings, endless optimization checks, and multi-tasking on every dimension of your enterprise, you're implementing a recipe for exhaustion, not exponential growth. Building mental resilience is about treating your brain with the same respect you'd give a high-performance race car: it needs maintenance, time in the pit, and a steady flow of fuel.

Let's use an airline metaphor: As they say, "Put on your own oxygen mask first." That doesn't mean you're selfish. It means ensuring that the only person propelling the business forward— you—is primed to deliver and sustain high-level output.

Burnout-Proof Practices for Solo Builders:

- **Guard Your Mornings:** The first 30 minutes set mental momentum for the day. Anchor them with inspiring inputs—whether it's journaling, reading, or strategic thinking.
- **Time Blocking Recovery:** Schedule short breaks with the same priority as meetings. Block 15-minute windows for stretching, meditating, or simply unplugging.
- **The 80% Rule:** On days when you feel frayed, commit to giving 80% on purpose. Why? You're choosing resilience over perfectionism.

The Lesson: A burned-out entrepreneur builds nothing. Protect your mind like you're CEO of your mental energy.

5. Cultivating Visionary Belief: The Unicorn Mindset

Here's a blunt truth: No one will believe in your idea more than you do. If you doubt its viability, so will investors, customers, and even your friends.

Great solo founders operate from visionary belief. Steve Jobs wasn't Steve Jobs because he created the iPhone; he was Steve Jobs because in 1984, when most people didn't even own a personal computer, he believed he could redefine the human experience. His unshakable belief wasn't an arrogant delusion; it was an alignment between his vision and his actions.

Such visionary belief starts by shifting how you hold your enterprise in your mind:

- **Affirmation Frameworks:** Craft positive assertions about your business, spoken aloud, as if it already exists. Example: "Millions use my software because it solves a need with joy and simplicity."
- **The Inner Board of Directors:** Surround yourself with the internal voices of mentors, real or imagined. When making decisions, ask yourself, "What would my greatest mentor (alive or dead) do here?"

One more thing: belief isn't blind. It's fostered by creating a feed-forward loop of smaller successes that reinforce big visions. Start by setting one hyper-specific, achievable goal. For example, instead of obsessing over making your product a household name, focus next quarter on converting 100 loyal customers. That micro-victory fortifies your confidence like stepping stones across a seemingly infinite river.

CONCLUSION

THE UNICORN YOU'VE BUILT—AND THE JOURNEY AHEAD

You've reached the end of this book, but your journey is just beginning. Along the way, we've explored the tools, strategies, and mindset shifts required to build a single-handed unicorn in the age of artificial intelligence. You now have the blueprint—a systematic approach to identifying opportunities, automating processes, and scaling your vision into something extraordinary.

But let's pause for a moment. What you've learned isn't just about AI or business; it's about something far greater. It's about the power of belief—belief in your ability to act, adapt, and create in ways you never thought possible.

The tools we've discussed—AI platforms, no-code solutions, automated systems—are just that: tools. They are only as powerful as the person using them. And that's where the real magic lies: *you.* It's your courage, your creativity, and your willingness to step into uncertainty that will transform an idea into a reality.

Think back to the beginning of this book. Maybe you felt intimidated by the vast horizon in front of you, unsure whether you had the skills or resources to make this journey. Now, I hope you see that the horizon wasn't an obstacle—it was an invitation. An invitation to dream bigger, take bold action, and rewrite the rules of what's possible.

Your Next Steps

As you close this book, I challenge you to reflect on a few key questions:

- What will you create with the knowledge and tools you now possess?
- What impact will your unicorn have on the people, industries, or communities around you?
- How will you stay resilient when challenges arise?

Remember, the path of a single-handed unicorn builder isn't about perfection—it's about progress. It's about taking the first step, then the next, and learning as you go.

You don't need a perfect plan. You don't need the certainty of success. All you need is the willingness to start.

A FINAL THOUGHT

The future belongs to those who dare to create it. In a world where technology is leveling the playing field, the difference between those who build unicorns and those who don't isn't access to resources—it's the willingness to act.

So take a deep breath, open your laptop, and begin. Your single-handed unicorn is waiting to be built—not by someone else, but by you.

The horizon is yours. Now go claim it.

ABOUT THE AUTHOR

Tim Cortinovis is a bestselling author, entrepreneur, and international speaker recognized as a Top 10 Thought Leader in Agentic AI and a Top 50 Thought Leader in Entrepreneurship by Thinkers360. With four bestselling books to his name, Tim has been inspiring and guiding business leaders since 2011.

A sought-after keynote speaker and workshop facilitator, Tim travels globally—speaking in English, German, and Spanish—to help startups and enterprises harness the power of cutting-edge technologies like AI, the metaverse, and blockchain for exponential growth. Among his clients are startups and Fortune 500 companies seeking to leverage cutting-edge technologies for growth.

The quickest way to find Tim is on LinkedIn, where he posts (almost) daily insights into new technologies in sales and responds to his DMs.

ALSO FROM TIM CORTINOVIS:

"Selling Smarter, Not Harder: How Sales Leaders Use Generative AI For Sales Excellence"

"A Game-Changer for Sales Professionals!" - Bruce Diamond

"Great guide how AI changes good selling techniques." Jamie

Generative AI is all around us. But which tool, which method really works for us in sales?

In "Selling Smarter, Not Harder: The Generative AI Playbook for Sales Excellence," Tim Cortinovis, recently named Thought Leader 100 Artificial Intelligence, takes you on a transformative journey into the heart of AI-driven sales.

You'll dive into a world where data overwhelm, cutthroat competition, and the incessant demand for efficiency and personalization reign supreme. It's a landscape where many sales teams struggle, not for lack of effort, but for lack of the right tools and strategies. That's where "Selling Smarter, Not Harder" comes in.

This isn't just another book about automation; it's a blueprint for elevating your sales process to an art form where technology amplifies your human strengths. You'll learn how to marry your creativity and emotional intelligence with AI's predictive analytics and efficiency, creating a sales force that's unstoppable.

 Available as:

Ebook
Paperback, 225 pages
Buy the book on Amazon

Together with Oliver Leisse:

"The Age of Agents: The Next Dimension of The Internet"

Search is shifting from classical search engines to chatbots and other agents, making search as comfortable and fast as possible. More and more AI agents are emerging. We see tourist agents searching for flights and booking them on our behalf.

The internet develops into its next dimension. This book is your companion to understanding this fundamental change and to be prepared.

Nothing, from information gathering to online shopping to education and advanced training, will ever be the same.

Available as:

ebook
Paperback, 225 pages
Buy the book on Amazon

Make your event impressive, hire Tim as a speaker in English, Spanish and German

Check Tim´s availability
post@cortinovis.de

Rick (WhatsApp)
https://wa.me/494060770255

Messenger https://m.me//TimCortinovis/)

Spread the word

If you got inspired by this book please tell the world and leave a review on Amazon!

Made in United States
Orlando, FL
18 February 2025

58661045R00108